D1450422

The Power of Positive Coaching

"Lee and Julie deliver powerful lessons with simple, concise language. As inspirational as it is practical. A vital tool for leaders at any career stage. An extraordinary book!"

Dr. Marshall Goldsmith
The Thinkers50 #1 Leadership Thinker in the World

"Lee Colan keeps it simple and impactful! His employee engagement concepts have been deeply embedded into our organization for years. I am excited to apply these practical coaching concepts and tools from *The Power of Positive Coaching*, and I have no doubt they will benefit our legacy company for years to come."

Frank Dulcich
President and CEO,
Pacific Seafood Group

"Leaders everywhere would derive great rewards from the specific, impactful, and helpful guidance that Lee and Julie deliver on effective coaching. *The Power of Positive Coaching* provides what all of us need to ensure that we nurture successful mentoring relationships and effectively steward the next generation of leaders in our organizations and communities."

Charles L. Iacovou
Sisel Distinguished Dean of the School of Business,
Wake Forest University

"*The Power of Positive Coaching* describes the daily challenge of coaching in simple terms and brings it to life with engaging examples. The authors' encouraging style and practical tools empower leaders to take positive action for their teams . . . and inspire positive results."

Daniel L. Jones
President and CEO,
Encore Wire Corporation

"This book has a great effort-to-impact ratio. *The Power of Positive Coaching* is an easy, engaging read while it cuts through the clutter to deliver impactful tools. It resonates with new and seasoned leaders to help them elevate their coaching game."

Kevin McManus

Head of Sales, North America Services, SAP America, Inc.

"The authors cracked the coaching code! They simplified the art of coaching into five easily communicated and applied steps. Thank you, Lee, for being an inspiring leader and coach!"

Jerry L. Crawford

CEO, Jani-King International, Inc.

"Lee Colan and Julie Davis-Colan provide a timely and relevant book every leader and aspiring leader should read. As the authors so aptly point out, 'You must get your mind right before you can get your team right.' A good first step would be to read this book."

Joel T. Allison

Senior Advisor to the Robbins Institute for Health
Policy and Leadership, Baylor University

"The authors know it's not about complex competencies or innate skills—it's about the simple and clear things we THINK and DO every day. No scripts or flow charts to remember—just powerful tips and behaviors paired with proven tools to boost team performance."

Dean Carter

Vice President, Human Resources and Shared Services,
Patagonia

"After almost 20 years of being coached by Lee on many of these principles, I am thankful that he has put them in writing. As a coaches' coach, Lee delivers great and practical insights to help every leader be a better coach. Consistent with their previous books, Lee and Julie write to the point and deliver practical tools that leaders can apply immediately."

Barry E. Davis

Executive Chairman, EnLink Midstream

"Three cheers to Lee and Julie. They've done it again! The Colans are reliably inspirational and practical! When they speak, I listen."

Denis G. Simon

Senior Executive Vice President,
Challenger, Gray & Christmas, Inc.

"Lee Colan really, really gets it. He has a unique skill of converting complex leadership concepts into an easy-to-understand, practical approach. He has done it again in *The Power of Positive Coaching*. His blend of experience and know-how is hard to find. If you want engaged, or better yet, inspired leaders—he is the man!"

Dave Loeser
Chairman and Executive Vice President,
New Day Financial

"*The Power of Positive Coaching* is a handy field guide for every leader. The authors deliver simple but powerful tools that you can put to work with your team right away. It is a quick-read, high-impact resource!"

Terry Looper
CEO, Texon LP

"I have enjoyed and applied Lee and Julie Colan's leadership ideas for years. *The Power of Positive Coaching* is an instant classic! This book presents simple coaching strategies that feel accessible and actionable. As a result, I feel better equipped to lead my team with the right mindset and the right habits."

Valerie Freeman
CEO, Imprimis Group

"Colan always finds the right balance of inspiring and equipping his readers, audiences, and clients. I have benefited in all three categories. *The Power of Positive Coaching* is on point again. It compellingly presents timely research and timeless strategies that are relevant and actionable for any leader."

Dr. Stephen L. Mansfield, FACHE
President and CEO, Methodist Health System

"Ever since I met Lee Colan and read his and Julie's book, *Sticking to It: The Art of Adherence*, I have been a fan. Their ability to reduce the complexity of leadership to a simple, concise set of habits and principles sets them apart. Even more importantly, by reading this book, a good leader can become an excellent leader by focusing on their five coaching habits. Any team and company will benefit by implementing the reliability advantage."

Dennis McCuistion
Television host and Executive Director, The Institute for
Excellence in Corporate Governance,
The University of Texas at Dallas

"Lee and Julie articulate that great leaders choose to meet the needs of their team over any personal discomforts. This choice is made through first knowing yourself and then having clarity in establishing priorities in business and life. I highly recommend this leadership journey for anyone who wants to improve themselves and their team."

Craig Dunaway
President, Penn Station East Coast Subs

"Lee has written another insightful coaching book that will be an excellent resource for new or seasoned business leaders. I've utilized Lee's talents and tools over the years. Whether coaching new or experienced leaders, I've found Lee's coaching style and methods to be extremely effective. Well done!"

Chuck Jerasá
Group President, Gibraltar Industries

"*The Power of Positive Coaching* is EXCELLENT! What a fantastic reminder of the fundamental value of a positive mindset and habits, personally and as a coach to your team. This is clearly the most straightforward and immediately usable treatment of this topic available today."

Scott C. Florence
Sales Vice President, AdvoCare International

"Positivity is, indeed, the most fundamental element of differentiation. The authors have captured this essential ingredient and incorporated the steps for winning in *The Power of Positive Coaching*. The book itself has achieved differentiation through actionable advice you can count on!"

Jim Keyes
Former CEO, 7-Eleven and Blockbuster

"*The Power of Positive Coaching* is filled with powerful insights and practical tips. It's a must-have guide for leaders at all levels. Kudos to Lee and Julie for providing yet another powerful tool for the leader's toolbox!"

Sharon Goldstein
Campus Operating Officer, Berkeley College Online

Other Books by the Authors

107 Ways to Stick to It: Practical Tips to
Achieve the Success You Deserve

• • •

7 Moments . . . That Define Excellent Leaders

• • •

Engaging Minds and Hearts of All Your Employees: How to
Ignite Passionate Performance for Better Business Results

• • •

Getting the BEST from Yourself and Others:
How to Orchestrate Your Attitude

• • •

Inspire! Connecting with Students to Make a Difference

• • •

Leadership Matters: Daily Insights to
Inspire Extraordinary Results

• • •

Orchestrating Attitude: Getting the
Best from Yourself and Others

• • •

Power Exchange: How to Boost Accountability
and Performance in Today's Workforce

• • •

Stick with It: Mastering the Art of Adherence

• • •

The 5 Coaching Habits of Excellent Leaders:
How to Create the Reliability Advantage for Your Team

• • •

The Nature of Excellence

• • •

Winners Always Quit: Seven Pretty Good Habits
You Can Swap for Really Great Results

The Power
of
Positive
Coaching

The Power

of

Positive

Coaching

The Mindset and Habits to Inspire
Winning Results and Relationships

Lee J. Colan, PhD

Julie Davis-Colan

New York Chicago San Francisco Athens London Madrid
Mexico City Milan New Delhi Singapore Sydney Toronto

1 2 3 4 5 6 7 8 9   QFR   23 22 21 20 19 18

ISBN: 978-1-260-14272-3
MHID: 1-260-14272-8

e-ISBN: 978-1-260-14273-0
e-MHID: 1-260-14273-6

This publication is designed to provide accurate and authoritative information in regard to the subject matter covered. It is sold with the understanding that neither the author nor the publisher is engaged in rendering legal, accounting, securities trading, or other professional services. If legal advice or other expert assistance is required, the services of a competent professional person should be sought.
—*From a Declaration of Principles Jointly Adopted by a Committee of the American Bar Association and a Committee of Publishers and Associations*

McGraw-Hill Education books are available at special quantity discounts to use as premiums and sales promotions or for use in corporate training programs. To contact a representative, please visit the Contact Us pages at www.mhprofessional.com.

CONTENTS

FOREWORD
by Dr. Marshall Goldsmith

For those of us in the coaching arena who help others change their lives for the better, a positive outlook is imperative. Lee Colan and Julie Davis-Colan bring this fact to light and explore the importance of our mindset and habits as coaches to inspire our clients to get better, enjoy great results, and have better relationships.

Today, with all the pressures of life and work, we're busier and working harder than we ever have. Sometimes life can be difficult, things happen that we don't like, and we get down. This is just a fact. As a coach, this can have a hugely detrimental effect on your team. If you aren't living a happy, healthy life, how can you expect your team to?

I take a cue from my wonderful friend Frances Hesselbein (former CEO of the Girl Scouts and recipient of the Presidential Medal of Freedom), who has a saying that I love. She says, when asked what her blood type is, "Be Positive!" This is her philosophy and it helps her navigate challenges in a positive way.

I love her outlook and I look for it in others as I travel around the world. How do people meet challenges and view change in a positive way? Here are some of the comments I've heard from friends, leaders, coaches, and students about how to view and manage difficulties in a positive and constructive way.

- "There is no use dwelling on the past. In hindsight, would I have done some things differently? Of course! I cannot change that now. I am focused on creating a great future."
- "In a strange way, my recent 'disasters' have made me better. I now realize that what matters is my health, friends, and family. I am grateful for the fact that I now understand what really matters."
- "I have a good job. I used to gripe about all kinds of minor annoyances at work. I recognize now that there are a lot of people out there who are much worse off than I am. All the little things that bothered me so much don't matter anymore."
- "I have time to invest in my future. I am using it to do what I always said I wanted to do. I am glad that I have a chance to do this."
- "My family is closer than ever. Some of us aren't doing so well. We are doing whatever we can to help each other. We love each other and support each other when times are tough."

Personally, I'm very grateful to have the opportunity to communicate with you, the readers of this wonderful book. And, I want to share with you that I am so thankful to continually learn from you and such exceptional and insightful authors as Lee and Julie. I hope that you will take the teachings of this book to heart and elevate your coaching game!

Life is good.

Dr. Marshall Goldsmith

Elevate Your Coaching Game

*Everyone needs a coach.
It doesn't matter whether you're a
basketball player, a tennis player,
a gymnast, or a bridge player.*

—BILL GATES
FOUNDER, MICROSOFT

t wasn't too long ago that having a business coach was like having a scarlet letter on your professional suit. Back then, most coaching was remedial—there was a problem that needed to be fixed. Today, having a coach has been elevated in status. Business leaders have realized what professional athletes have always known—having a coach produces better results. That's a significant and necessary paradigm shift. Instead of symbolizing a problem, having a coach symbolizes a leader's willingness to develop and grow as a person and a leader.

Research from the Korn Ferry Institute supports this paradigm shift in perceptions about coaching. The research found that most people rate "coaching and developing others" among the top three most important leadership competencies, according to 360-degree assessments. Although this competence is *rated* highly, it is consistently the least *practiced* competency worldwide. Why does this knowing/doing gap exist? Leaders say it is because they do not have enough time; they do not know a proven process; and/or they feel it will slow down their immediate performance.[1] These reasons—dare we say excuses—carry serious risks. If you don't take the time to coach and develop team members now, you will pay for it later—guaranteed. Using a haphazard, gut-feel coaching approach, only when it is convenient, yields haphazard results. If you neglect coaching to drive short-term results, you will handicap your team's ability to sustain performance over time. Coaching your team is the ultimate pay-me-now or pay-me-later leadership proposition. Applying a consistent approach to coaching others is fundamental to leadership excellence today.

A commitment to coaching also signals an organization's willingness to invest in its people. In today's environment of high-velocity change, factors like technology, product innovation, and unique distribution channels are fleeting advantages. In fact, the only *sustainable* competitive advantage is an organization's talent and how well that talent delivers its product or service. The coaching value chain directly links a leader's ability to coach his or her team with sustained growth and profitability:

Inspiring leaders coach teams to
   Build winning relationships internally and externally and
      Generate winning results that
         Produce sustained growth and profits.

Unfortunately, not every organization has the resources to hire external coaches. Therefore, it's critical for business leaders to be equipped as effective and inspiring coaches to their teams. We wrote this book to help you elevate your coaching game with an easy-to-apply approach, communicated in simple terms and supported with actionable tools. We have been privileged to have helped more than 100,000 leaders elevate their coaching games since 1999. Our passion is helping leaders become better coaches who inspire levels of performance their teams could not achieve by themselves.

> *The central role of a leader is that of a coach.*

Real-Time Coaching

We love watching the Olympics. In fact, we were thrilled when they started alternating the summer and winter

Olympics, so we would only have to wait two years instead of four years to see the games. The Olympics embody all that is good and inspiring about the human spirit. We are in awe of how these athletes practice day in and day out, week in and week out, year in and year out for that one moment to perform when it really matters.

As we watched the most recent Olympics, we had an aha moment. Olympians spend 99 percent of their time practicing, while they perform just one percent (or less) of the time. Your team members have the opposite challenge. They must perform 99 percent (or more) of the time taking care of customers, analyzing reports, developing their teams, generating sales, etc. In business, there is precious little time for your team to "practice" all these tasks. The vast majority of your team's learning and development happens on the job rather than in formal development programs.

Those who coach Olympic athletes literally spend years training their athletes during practice and typically can only sit and watch as they perform. Business coaches, on the other hand, have the opportunity to coach their team members, day in and day out for years, *in real time as they perform*. That is a powerful distinction.

Even though we are hardly Olympic athletes, we experience the power of a coach to elevate performance in real time whenever we go to an exercise class (Zumba® dance for Julie and TITLE® Boxing for Lee). The moment the trainer/coach walks within eyesight, we predictably elevate our intensity, exert more energy, and check to ensure our form is correct. This predictable and natural human reaction has been long established. In fact, the first study to demonstrate this effect was conducted by Norman Triplett, a psychologist from Indiana University, way back in 1898.[2] The fact that we perform better when we are coached in real time is referred to as *social facilitation*, which is defined as "an improvement in performance produced by the mere presence of others."

> *All coaching is, is taking a player where he can't take himself.*
>
> **—BILL McCARTNEY**
> Former American College Football Coach and President, Promise Keepers

Do you coach your team in real time? Imagine the performance improvement if you consistently instructed and encouraged your team daily *while* they were performing their jobs. What are the possibilities for offering feedback, adjusting on the fly, tweaking execution, changing plans mid-game? Doesn't your team deserve an engaged, inspiring coach to help them realize their full potential?

Power of the Positive

We have all seen different types of coaches in action. The angry, red-faced coaches who yell at their teams for their failures; the disengaged, flat-line coaches who are physically present but not actively engaged in coaching; and the positive, exciting coaches who inspire their teams to strive for more despite the circumstances. Which type of coaching produces the best results?

The benefits of positive coaching carry "face validity," meaning that even without research evidence, most people would agree that positive coaching generates real benefits (although as you'll see in the next chapter, there is plenty of research to support the validity of positive coaching). People in general, regardless of generation or culture, respond better to positive interactions. We do more for those who appreciate us and invest in us simply because it feels good. Since we are creatures of pleasure, we repeat the behavior that created that good feeling. This creates a self-perpetuating cycle of reinforced positive behavior and positive results. As we see too frequently, an equally powerful negative cycle can be created. Although some leaders argue that a negative response motivates people to perform, it also creates anxiety and triggers disengagement. A negative approach to coaching

> *A positive attitude causes a chain reaction of positive thoughts, events, and outcomes. It is a catalyst and it sparks extraordinary results.*
>
> **—WADE BOGGS**
> Hall of Fame Professional Baseball Player

typically does not sustain long-term performance because people respond to negative leadership with compliance versus commitment. To be clear, we are not saying to avoid tough conversations. Rather, we recommend coaching for performance improvement with a positive mindset and habits to increase the chances of positive results.

Positive coaching is not a soft approach. To the contrary, it leverages insights about human dynamics and performance to generate hard results. Positive coaching leads to:

- More focused effort (and less wasted mental and physical energy) because you and your team are aligned on expectations.
- More discretionary effort from your team because they are fully engaged.
- More ownership behavior and innovation because your team is involved in creating solutions.
- Greater accountability because your team knows their personal performance score.
- Deeper commitment from team members because your team feels genuinely appreciated and valued.

The results are a more productive team, improved relationships, and sustained positive performance.

Positive Mindset and Habits

Inspiring winning results and relationships is a two-dimensional challenge that involves a positive coaching mindset and positive coaching habits. Having either one is insufficient to equip leaders to coach effectively and inspire their teams optimally. Most coaching books and workshops focus on skills and habits, which are essential. You can perform all the right skills, but without the right mindset those skills and habits will not yield the response and results you want from your team. On the other hand, the right mindset is crucial, but without corresponding coaching habits, you will never see that mindset translated into coaching behaviors. A positive coaching mindset and positive coaching habits go hand in hand, and they have more than a proportional relationship. Your coaching mindset has a multiplier effect on your coaching habits. This relationship between mindset and habits can be expressed in a simple equation:

Positive Coaching Mindset

×

Positive Coaching Habits

=

Winning Results and Relationships

Business coaching is an inside job. It starts with your knowledge and clarity of who you are; then it emanates

8

outward to your coaching skills and habits. In the first part of this book we will discuss the four levels of knowledge that build a positive coaching mindset. Your mindset will either limit or expand the possibilities and results you will achieve by applying the coaching habits. That's why we will address your mindset first. Next, we will outline the five positive coaching habits—the skill set—with supporting tools for each one. Equipped with a positive coaching mindset and positive coaching habits, you can inspire winning results and relationships.

Investing in your team produces a positive return just like the interest you earn on a financial investment. And like a financial investment, your investment in others compounds over time. Start investing in your team today. Every day you miss is a performance loss that you cannot recoup. In the words of Zig Ziglar, an inspiring coach to millions, "You don't have to be great to start, but you have to start to be great." So, let's get started.

> *Perpetual optimism is a force multiplier.*
>
> **—COLIN POWELL,**
> U.S. Army General

PART I

Positive Coaching Mindset

> *You must get your mind right before you can get your team right.*
>
> —JULIE DAVIS-COLAN

Your mindset has significant influence on how you perform, lead, and coach. Psychologist Carol Dweck asserts, based on decades of research, that how we see ourselves is a major factor in what we ultimately achieve.[1] You will rise to the level of expectations of yourself. What is your current mindset? Do you think you can change, improve, achieve, lead, and coach with excellence?

Your mindset also has a dramatic impact on those you coach. People rise to the level of your expectations for them. A recent study by Korn Ferry Institute found that 65 percent of female chief executive officers (CEOs) from large companies realized they could be a CEO only after someone told them they could be a CEO.[2] At first glance, this statistic might seem shocking. But consider how often you have observed an average employee under an average leader begin to flourish once he or she is assigned to an inspiring leader who sees the potential in that employee. Just like these female CEOs, you and those you coach will rise to the level of expectations. Your mindset about yourself and others is one of the very best predictors of the winning results and relationships you will inspire. It is the coach's mindset and expectations that make all the difference.

Assume the Best

It is a common design principle to build systems and plans for the norm instead of for the exception. So why not design your mindset the same way?

To embrace a positive coaching mindset, assume the best of others. If you choose to protect yourself from disappointment by always thinking the worst, you have also chosen disappointment as the filter through which you view all things and people . . . and that's just what you will get. Alternatively, you can choose to think the best all the time. Choose to make a positive mindset your norm. Sure, you might be disappointed occasionally but, most of the time, you will be programming your mind and others to achieve their best.

Your mindset predisposes you to see behaviors that reinforce your mindset, negative or positive. No doubt, your employees can be frustrating and noncompliant at times. That's why it is so important to bring a positive mindset into the relationship. If your mindset is, "This team member is difficult and not collaborative," you are already predisposed to look for, and predictably find, behaviors that reinforce this negative mindset. If your mindset is, "I think this employee can stretch herself and really lead this project successfully," you will likely look for and find skills and behaviors that support your mindset. This is known as *confirmation bias*, which is the tendency to search for, interpret, favor, and recall information in a way that confirms your preexisting beliefs.

As a coach, consider what you will see and the different outcomes you can expect if you choose the positive coaching mindset on the left versus the negative one on the right.

POSITIVE MINDSET		NEGATIVE MINDSET
She can change and grow.	vs.	She is stuck in her ways.
He has not mastered this yet.	vs.	He just doesn't get it.
He really wants to succeed.	vs.	He just wants a paycheck.
He wants to do the right thing.	vs.	He will probably cheat and steal for his own benefit.
She wants to help.	vs.	She just cares about herself.
She has several natural gifts.	vs.	She has several weaknesses.

Researchers illustrated the power of mindset by proving that managers who used a strength-based approach with their employees helped to improve employee performance by 36.4 percent. On the other hand, managers who focused primarily on the employees' weaknesses helped to decrease their employees' performance by 26.8 percent.[3] If you are committed to winning

> *Your mindset today directly influences your results and relationships tomorrow.*

15

results and relationships, then choosing a positive coaching mindset is an easy choice because it is the only choice.

Positivity Broadens Possibilities

Does a positive mindset actually make a difference in your coach approach and effectiveness? The answer is an emphatic yes! The field of positive psychology has blossomed with practical findings over the past decade. Research by Barbara L. Fredrickson, for example, reveals that positive thoughts help you see more options and solutions for solving problems, a skill set which is at the core of an inspiring coach and winning teams.[4]

Our brains respond to negative emotions by limiting the options we consider. For example, when you're in a conflict with a colleague or a loved one, your anger and frustration might consume you to the point where you can't think about anything else. Also, if you are feeling stressed and overwhelmed with a long to-do list, you might find it hard to take one small action to get started. Your negative emotions can prevent your brain from seeing the other options and choices that surround you.

Fredrickson tested the impact of positive emotions on the brain by dividing her research subjects into five groups and showing each group film clips. The first two groups were shown clips that elicited positive emotions;

the third group saw images that were neutral; and the last two groups saw clips that created negative emotions. Then, each participant was asked to imagine themselves in a situation where they would experience similar emotions and write down what they would do.

Fascinatingly, participants who saw negative emotions wrote down the fewest responses. Meanwhile, the participants who experienced positive emotions wrote down a significantly higher number of actions, even when compared to the control group. The results revealed that when you experience positive emotions, you see more possibilities. This has big implications for leaders. The coach with a positive mindset is better able to see more opportunities for growth and improvement. Plus, the employee who is being coached is better equipped to solve problems and expand his or her capabilities as a result of being coached with a positive mindset.

Building a Coaching Mindset

Our company logo is a group of three stacked L's, which represent the three levels of leadership: personal, team, and organizational. The logo represents our belief that personal leadership drives team leadership which in turn drives organizational leadership. Excellence, like leadership, is built from the inside out. Your organization's

> *Your mindset . . .*
> *Reflects*
> *your past,*
> *Describes your*
> *present, and*
> *Predicts your*
> *future.*

excellence will rarely exceed your team's excellence, and your team's excellence will rarely exceed your personal excellence. Therefore, the most important question a leader should ask is: "What am I currently doing to improve my personal excellence?" Inspiring coaches work on themselves before they work on their teams. It starts inside with an understanding of yourself. A positive coaching mindset is built on a foundation of self-knowledge. Inspiring coaches intentionally, courageously, and consistently deepen four levels of self-awareness to build a positive coaching mindset:

1. Know Your Thoughts
2. Know Your Purpose
3. Know Your Values
4. Know Your Emotions

Keen awareness at these four levels enables you to be more personally effective, authentic, and credible. Just as importantly, seeking greater self-awareness creates a culture that is conducive to coaching and a team that is more responsive to your coaching.

Watch your thoughts;
they become your words.
Watch your words;
they become your actions.
Watch your actions;
they become your habits.
Watch your habits;
they become your character.
Watch your character;
it becomes your destiny.

—FRANK OUTLAW
Founder, BI-LO supermarket chain

CHAPTER 1

Know Your Thoughts

Change your thoughts and
you change your world.

—NORMAN VINCENT PEALE
AUTHOR, *THE POWER OF POSITIVE THINKING*

The greatest form of knowledge is knowing your-self. Knowing yourself starts with knowing your thoughts. Your mindset is nothing more than a compilation of your thoughts. Your thoughts have incredible power to shape your life and the lives of others, because your thoughts and interpretations of circumstances directly influence your beliefs, and ultimately, your actions. Henry Ford said, "Whether you think you can or cannot, you're right." In other words, what you think is what you get. That is why it is critical that you know your thoughts.

You draw into your life that which you constantly think about—good or bad. If you are always thinking about why you can't seem to get a break, or when the next shoe will drop in your relationship, or why you don't get as much recognition as your colleague, then you are programming your mind (and those around you) to turn these thoughts into your reality. Negative thoughts are landmines along the pathway to being your best. Fortunately, the reverse is also true. If you consistently and intentionally nurture positive thoughts and expectations, you paint a picture of future success on the walls of your mind. Some people ask, "How can I be positive when negative situations are a reality—they just show up in everyday life?" Bad things do happen and they sometimes "just show up." However, it is your interpretation that makes a situation negative. A situation doesn't drag you down or lift you up, but the way you think about it does.

The great news is that you are in control of what you think. No one else has this power unless you give it away. You are the conductor of your own thoughts. Inspiring coaches choose to understand, control, and change their thoughts to form a positive mindset, which helps them elevate their coaching game.

Your Ultimate Computer

Your mind is your ultimate personal computer. Just like your laptop at home, sometimes you might forget to turn on your mental virus protection program, allowing negative inputs to invade your mind without even realizing it. The old computer database adage "Garbage in, garbage out" as it applies to your mind should really be "Garbage in, garbage stays." Whatever your mind hears from others, and especially from you, it records and files away. If you hear something often enough, you will tend to believe it and act upon it. Unfortunately, the mind doesn't discriminate between input that is good for you or harmful to you; it collects and stores *all* input. Consider three of the most common sources of input into your thought life. They have the potential for a positive or negative impact on your thoughts, and ultimately, your results: other people, media, and you.

Choose to surround yourself with people who offer positive input. The best strategy is to make a conscious effort to get to know and spend time with people who have a positive outlook and offer you constructive input. Notice that we use the word "constructive." *Constructive input* is presented with positive intentions, although constructive input might still feel uncomfortable to receive. The key is that it is meant to build you up versus break you down. There will always be negative people and perspectives. Since you cannot hide from them, learn to filter out nonconstructive input to minimize "garbage" in your thoughts. Fred Smith was a student at Yale University when he submitted a paper about the impact of a computerized society and the changes he envisioned for traditional distribution and delivery systems. It is reported that Smith's professor returned the paper commenting, "The concept is interesting and well-formed, but in order to earn better than a 'C,' the idea must be feasible." Just five years later Smith figured out a way to make it feasible and named his company Federal Express. He filtered the negative input from his professor and chose to seek out more positive input, and ultimately, a positive outcome.

Media is omnipresent in today's world. Your cell phone, computer, billboards as you drive, the floor tiles in the grocery store, banners at a ballgame, taglines on a t-shirt—we take in media impressions minute by minute instead of only during the evening news in pre-Internet days. The subconscious mind is most receptive five minutes before you doze off at night, still a common time for watching the broadcast news on television.

Unfortunately, much of the news today shows the worst side of people and the world. When you hear a news story, remind yourself that it's considered news because it is *unusual*. Doing so will help you balance potentially negative input with more uplifting thoughts.

So how can you remain well informed and maintain a positive outlook? Monitor what you watch. Make the choice to watch more programs that are educational, artistic, spiritual, or sports- and comedy-oriented. These types of programs stimulate positive thoughts. Before you start reading or watching a news feed or broadcast, take a quick inventory of all the things you are grateful for. Additionally, make it a habit to finish your reading with an inspiring story so that your mind is primed for a positive day.

The most important and pervasive source of input is you. No one is with you as much as you are. You have an opportunity every day to consciously give yourself positive input and reinforce your own positive actions. Julie has a practice of giving herself mental high fives. That is, she frequently tells herself (often out loud), "Great job, Julie!" You talk with many people each day, but the most important conversation is the one you have with yourself.

Your mind can be your greatest ally or your worst enemy. Input from others, media, and yourself plants expectational seeds of success or failure in your mind. Seek positive inputs and you will improve your chances of producing positive outputs and responses. The choice is yours.

Look for Cannoli

We have a special family tradition with our children. For their 12th birthday, they can select any city in the continental United States to visit for a special celebration with just Mom and Dad, with no siblings. Our middle child decided on New York City to celebrate her 12th birthday. Having been there many times ourselves, it was fun to see the wonderment in a first-time visitor's eyes as she took in the lights of Times Square, the windows of the shops along Fifth Avenue, the view from the Empire State Building, and the ethnic richness of Chinatown and Little Italy.

Since our hotel was near Times Square, we walked a well-worn path down Broadway during our stay. Times Square really is the ultimate in sensory overload. During nearly a dozen trips down the same street, we noticed something new every time. Whatever item we were looking for seemed to magically appear even though we had previously walked past it numerous times without noticing—a souvenir shop, a deli, a street vendor selling scarves, a hot dog stand, live musicians, or Italian cannoli.

This experience reminded us once again that the things we pay the most attention to reflect what we think about most. If we change what we think about, what we notice in our surroundings will change. We call this connection between our thoughts and our attention "The

Yellow Car Phenomenon." For example, when was the last time you saw a yellow car that wasn't a taxi? Maybe last week or last month? Now that we have made you aware of yellow cars and you are thinking about them, you will start seeing more of them. The same is true when you buy a new car; suddenly you see the same make, model, and color everywhere you look. Julie says the phenomenon also occurs for a pregnant woman; everywhere you look, you see other pregnant women. Is there a sudden invasion of pregnant women? Of course not; they've been there all along, and so have the yellow cars and the same make and model car you purchased. The difference is, because you are thinking about them, you more readily notice them.

This phenomenon is rooted in neuroscience. The reticular activating system (RAS) is the brain's filter between the subconscious mind and conscious mind. Without you being aware of it, the RAS sifts through the millions of pieces of information, stimuli, and data coming into your brain from all your senses. The RAS then filters out the irrelevant and brings only the relevant information to your conscious mind. So, the RAS decides what you put your attention toward, and allows your conscious mind to focus only on that which you've determined is useful right now. This explains why, on our walks down Broadway in New York City, we didn't notice the Italian cannoli when we were looking for scarves. But once we were hungry, we saw cannoli galore!

The things we focus on create a magnet for our lives. If we focus on the negative, we tend to see more negatives. For example:

- Focus on problems, and obstacles are plentiful.
- Focus on things outside of your control, and you will easily throw in the towel and give up in frustration.
- Focus on fear versus faith, and you will be paralyzed with inaction.
- Focus on weakness instead of strengths, and you will miss your natural giftedness.
- Focus on the drama that life offers, and your life will be a soap opera.

What does the RAS have to do with coaching? Inspiring coaches use "The Yellow Car Phenomenon" to focus on the positive:

- Focus on opportunities, and doors seem to open.
- Focus on forgiveness, and you will find the world forgiving.
- Focus on the comedy life offers, and your life will be full of laughs.
- Focus on what is going well, and you build your team's confidence.
- Focus on learning and moving forward, and stumbling blocks are converted into stepping-stones.

The world reflects your view of it, so if you change the way you look at things, things change the way they look. When coaching your team, look for "cannoli." In other words, look for the good stuff. The more you focus on the positive, the more you will create positive outcomes for you and your team.

> **We see what we look for.**

Check Your Blind Spot

Knowing your own tendencies, preferences, personal limits, natural gifts, and weaknesses helps you be more personally effective, and as a result, a more insightful, honest, and inspiring coach. You must know yourself to coach others most effectively.

Self-aware people and inspiring coaches intentionally work to minimize their blind spots. *Blind spots* are behaviors, traits, or tendencies that others see, but you are unaware of. Picture the friend who thinks he is a great listener, but everyone knows he just never shuts up.

Researchers David Zes and Dana Landis analyzed 6,977 assessments of managers and executives to identify blind spots. They compared the results to the financial data of the 486 publicly traded companies in which the subjects worked. After tracking stock performance over 30 months, the researchers found that organizations with a higher percentage of self-aware leaders (fewest blind spots) had the strongest financial performance. Companies with the least self-aware leaders (most blind spots) had the lowest financial performance.[1]

It is no coincidence that a leader's self-knowledge helps him or her lead and coach more effectively. This higher quality of coaching has a greater positive effect on the performance of the leader's team, which in turn creates a ripple effect throughout the organization. This ultimately reveals itself in winning results and relationships.

How can you become more self-aware of your blind spots? If you have taken a 360-degree assessment in the past, refer to the feedback report. It's a great place to start uncovering blind spots. Look for areas where you rated yourself significantly higher than your team or your team leader rated you. If you haven't taken a 360-degree assessment, the best way to minimize blind spots is to ask your team what you can *Start, Stop, and Keep* doing to help them succeed . . . and carefully listen to their answers. It is simple on the mind, but it can be tough on the heart. It takes courage to ask for feedback and potentially uncover blind spots, but the cost of low self-awareness is your leadership and coaching credibility.

> *Coaches have to watch for what they don't want to see and listen to what they don't want to hear.*
>
> **—JOHN MADDEN**
> Pro Football Hall of Fame Coach

Inspiring coaches *prevent* blind spots by making concerted efforts to listen for unfiltered truth about challenges, opportunities, and most importantly, about their leadership. This is particularly important because the higher you are in an organization, the more filtered the information you receive. It's a natural and predictable phenomenon, but it's also a precarious position to be in. No leader wants to be "the emperor who wore no clothes."

Create Mental Space

The blinding speed of today's information-saturated, time-deprived, hypercompetitive world forces us to run, run, run just to keep pace. Alarm! Hit snooze. Alarm! Shower. Shave. Turn cell phone on. Check headlines. Check voice mail. Check e-mail. Google dog groomer. Make dinner reservations. Microwave breakfast. Drive to office. Check e-mail. Check schedule. Text Junior about afternoon pickup time for soccer practice. Join global teleconference in progress. Answer incoming texts. And that's just the first hour.

Accessibility through technology can be a double-edged sword. It is a blessing in terms of your productivity, but it is a curse on your peace of mind and your ability to know yourself. You can end up being a "human doing" rather than a human being, which leaves no time for awareness. When you're busy being a "human doing," you're usually too focused on your job to look outside at the big picture or look inside at your thoughts.

So, how, exactly, in today's hyperactive and attention-demanding world, can you spend more time thinking about your thinking? Quit moving and be still. Relax. Be quiet. Look around. Listen. Our youngest daughter has a special area in her room where she can chill and relax. She calls it her "chillax zone." Although your "chillax zone" might not have big pink pillows and a fluffy white carpet, you also need to make a time and place that offers mental space. Your space can be your car as you drive home after work, a reading or meditation corner in your house, your bathtub, your gym, a nearby park where you walk; your space can be anywhere you can be alone with your thoughts. The thinking, planning, and reflection you do in this space helps you get off the treadmill and rise above the hurly-burly of your everyday world to gain a better perspective on yourself, your purpose, your values, your team, etc.

> *A quiet mind enhances our hearing.*

You don't have to go on vacation or head for the spa. All you have to do is change the scenery in your mind. Instead of trudging along the dusty trail following the ruts of the wagon train, fly yourself to the top of the mountain where you can be still, relax, and dream while you gaze out over the world below.

When you stop moving, your world gets quieter. You don›t hear the babble of people working all around you, the rustle of information, the pinging of emotion, the roar of the wind past your ears. All that noise is gone, and then you can truly listen. As Indira Gandhi said, "You must learn to be still in the midst of activity and to be vibrantly alive at rest." So, try being still to be more aware of your thoughts so you can intentionally form a positive coaching mindset.

CHAPTER 2

Know Your Purpose

*The first responsibility of a leader is to
define reality. The last is to say thank you.
In between, the leader is a servant.*

—MAX DE PREE
FORMER CEO, HERMAN MILLER, INC.; AUTHOR

Do you know what your purpose is as a leader, independent from your position or title?

Inspiring coaches view their purpose as service to others. They focus on how many people they serve versus how many people serve them. Inspiring coaches feel called to help good employees become better people. They build their employees from the inside out . . . inspiring excellence personally and professionally.

This means that the needs of others come first and that the team's success is a leader's claim to success. Inspiring coaches choose to meet the needs of their teams, despite any personal discomfort. It reminds us of our son's former high school football coach, Chris Cunningham, who preached this same leadership concept of "team over me." He even had t-shirts printed with a BIG "team" and a little tiny "me":

$$\frac{\text{TEAM}}{\text{me}}$$

In other words, the needs of your team are bigger than your needs as their leader. Your feelings must be subordinated to the demands of a higher cause—serving your team. To serve your team well, you must connect with and invest in them.

Connecting

As a leader and as a coach you have the opportunity and responsibility to encourage and support the *connections* that generate winning relationships and results. Lest you think "connecting" refers to being technologically connected (which most of us are all day, every day), let us clarify. We are talking about *connecting* with your team in authentic ways. The fact is that we live in a high-tech world, but creating real connections is still a high-touch job.

> *Successful people become great leaders when they learn to shift the focus from themselves to others.*
>
> **—DR. MARSHALL GOLDSMITH**
> Author, *What Got You Here Won't Get You There*

We recently saw a small, inspirational gift book that posed the question, "How does a child spell 'love'?" The book takes the reader through all the brief moments in a parent's life that are defining moments in a child's life. The moral of these moments is that a child spells "love" as T-I-M-E.[1] Your team spells it the same way.

Time is your most precious resource. You cannot manufacture it, and everyone has the same amount of it each day, from the chief executive officer to the frontline worker. If you want to serve, you must connect with your team, and if you want to connect, you must invest the time to build relationships. For example, one of our colleagues, a senior executive in the financial services industry, demonstrated her commitment to connect with a newly promoted manager. She considered this manager to be a high-potential individual who needed little of her time or supervision. Consequently, she asked him to provide an update 90 days after his promotion to see how he was doing. Well, her request for a 90-day update turned into 90 daily updates! But that did not sway our colleague's confidence in her newly promoted manager. She patiently gave her full attention to him during each daily update, because she recognized the value of connection. Her new manager simply wanted to ensure they were in sync. She knew that her time was of great value to this budding leader, so she willingly gave it to him. Today, she only gets the 90-day updates from this high-performing manager.

One of the fastest ways to connect with others is to find common ground, whether you are building a relationship or building a bridge to mend a relationship. When you really observe, watch, ask, and listen, it's easy to find things in common. Consider two people who are at odds and walk away from negotiations as a lost cause. Then a mediator walks in and quickly finds a win-win solution. The contentious parties are focusing on differences while the mediator is focused on commonalities. Use common ground as your "Yellow Car Phenomenon" and you will find abundant opportunities to connect.

Inspiring coaches excel not only at connecting directly with their team members, but also at helping team members connect with one another. We often hear people speak with envy about companies with "real heart," for example, Starbucks, Ben & Jerry's, Southwest Airlines, Harley-Davidson, Nordstrom, The Container Store, Apple,

FedEx, and Google. Outsiders are constantly looking for these companies' secrets to success. The "secret" is the connectedness within their teams. Their teams have strong connections that ignite strong passion that helps them deliver winning results.

In order to illustrate the power of connections, consider an experiment regarding the effects of relationships on group performance. This experiment compared the performance of groups of three friends to groups of three acquaintances. Each group was asked to follow specific instructions for building models made with Tinkertoy® pieces. The friends built an average of 9.0 models versus 2.45 models for the acquaintances. "[The friends] were able to challenge one another's ideas in a constructive way," said Karen Jehn, one of the researchers. "In the groups of acquaintances, people were almost too polite."[2]

So, what is the learning here? Connections among teammates increase engagement and productivity. These findings have been validated by other studies that show that strong connections and bonds among employees also enhance loyalty, retention, and job satisfaction.[3] Indeed, connections are the "secret" of winning organizations. Another compelling study demonstrates the practical power of connections. Researchers found that if a person is looking at a hill and judging how steep it is, the simple presence of a social support (friend) made the hill look 10 to 20 percent less steep than if the individual were alone.

You or your team's perception of a task, goal, or project is transformed for the better when the presence of others is felt on the journey to achievement.[4]

Investing

Although certain types of employee development require a financial investment (e.g., seminars, professional memberships, subscriptions), the best return is generated from an investment of your time and energy. Even though time and energy are always finite, purpose-driven leaders invest these precious resources into their teams. When employees know you have a vested interest in their success, tough discussions become easier, issues are addressed rather than avoided, and solutions are presented by rather than prodded from employees.

Andrew Carnegie was an excellent leader and inspiring coach. He came to America from his native Scotland when he was a small boy, did a variety of odd jobs, and eventually ended up as the largest steel manufacturer in the United States.

> *The HEIGHT of a team's performance compared to its potential is directly related to the DEPTH of connection among its members.*
>
> **—BARRY KAPLAN and JEFFREY MANCHESTER**
> Coauthors, *The Power of Vulnerability*

At one time, he was the wealthiest man in America. To put his wealth into perspective, he sold the Carnegie Steel Company to J. P. Morgan in 1901 for $480 million. Today's equivalent value is nearly $400 billion. Carnegie was also a great philanthropist. He donated the current equivalent of $79 billion to various charities, universities, and libraries.

At one point, Carnegie had 43 millionaires working for him. In the late 1800s, a millionaire was a very rare person. A reporter once asked Carnegie how he had managed to hire 43 millionaires. Carnegie responded that those people had not been millionaires when they started working for him, but rather had become millionaires as a result of working for him. The reporter's next question was: "How did you develop these men to become so valuable to you that you have paid them this much money?" Carnegie replied that men are developed the same way gold is mined. When gold is mined, several tons of dirt must be moved to get an ounce of gold, but one doesn't go into the mine looking for dirt—one goes in looking for the gold.

Inspiring coaches see it as their purpose to look for the gold in their employees. Once these coaches find it, they coach their employees to refine that gold. They help their employees build better lives for themselves and others while producing winning results. In the crunch of daily demands, it is easy to forget a fundamental law of leadership: If your employees are successful, you are successful.

Inspiring coaches are crystal clear on their purpose to invest in future leaders. This might look like:

- Letting team members shadow you at a meeting, even if others might not think they are quite ready for it.
- Sharing lessons learned and wisdom from your mentors, to help team members avoid mistakes you made and to enable them to succeed faster than you did.
- Reinforcing team members for good use of their natural gifts and creating opportunities for them to continue to use and hone those gifts.
- Having tough discussions to help reveal blind spots, so team members maintain good credibility with others.
- Connecting team members with internal or external people with different perspectives and expertise, to help broaden their understanding of your business and the industry.
- Discerningly delegating new tasks, to gradually stretch team members' skills and experiences. For example, when you return from a vacation or time away from the office, keep the expanded responsibilities you delegated in your absence as the new norm for the team member.

When we do good, we feel good. One of the most joyful moments for an inspiring coach is to pass the baton to someone you have invested in, and then see your purpose reflected in the new leader. We were meant to give away our lives. Focus on living your legacy instead of worrying about leaving your legacy. If you do, your leadership and your coaching will have true purpose.

> *A good coach can change a game. A great coach can change a life.*
>
> **—JOHN WOODEN**
> Former UCLA basketball coach and 10-time national champion

CHAPTER 3

Know Your Values

In matters of style, swim with the current;
in matters of principle, stand like a rock.

—THOMAS JEFFERSON
FOUNDING FATHER AND PRESIDENT
OF THE UNITED STATES

Being an inspiring coach is as much about who you are as it is about what you do. Your character is rooted in *your values*, those things that are vital to you and reflect your uniqueness and priorities. Your values, not your circumstances or fleeting feelings, should dictate your decisions and behavior. Your values about people and performance should guide your approach to coaching your team.

Personal values—like excellence, honesty, and openness—in and of themselves are just concepts and may be hard to put your finger on. However, once you convert those values into behaviors you can observe, then you can measure, manage, and live them. In this chapter, we will look at not only how you can convert your personal values into behaviors, but also how your personal values provide the framework for your team's values.

Common Values of Inspiring Coaches

Although choosing your values is certainly a personal matter, there are a few values inspiring coaches share:

Integrity: Without a doubt, your personal integrity is your most prized possession. Each day, that integrity is constantly tested, and you have an opportunity to prove it or lose it with every decision you make. If you compromise your integrity, your team will stop following you out of commitment and will follow you only out of compliance with your position. If people stop following you, you aren't really leading anymore, regardless of your title. Leading with integrity is not always the easiest thing to do, but it is always the right thing to do. Choosing to do the right thing—even when it's painful—ensures you will maintain your integrity throughout your personal and professional journey.

Humility: Coaching, in any venue, is about other people . . . not us. It's normal to feel proud of personal accomplishments, but inspiring coaches take more pride in their team's accomplishments than their own. Staying humble enables you to use your coaching platform to take a stand and conquer much more as a team than you could alone. True humility is expressed in your actions, not your words. You cannot afford to be like the guy who was voted most humble leader of a nationwide, professional association of leaders in the workforce. The association presented him with a medal that said, "Most Humble Leader in America." Then the association took it away from him at their next meeting because he wore the medal! Personal pride can turn into a slippery slope of egotism and arrogance. Build the courage to conquer the outside forces and the humility to conquer your inside forces.

Caring: The value of caring is expressed as a genuine interest in others. Inspiring coaches ask questions to get to know the person behind the employee. They do so not because they think they should, but because they really want to know their people and encourage them to be the best they can be. This deep caring is born out of the sense of purpose to serve others that these coaches feel, which we discussed in the prior chapter. Caring also means pay-ing attention—picking up on little signs, changes, moods, expressions and other cues—to gain a more complete pic-ture of the employee. Coaches who notice the little things can better help employees address root causes of chal-lenges, rather than just symptoms. Genuinely caring for your team also helps you manage your reactions because you are concerned about the other parties. We will address that topic in the next chapter.

What kind of coach do you want to be for your team? As you select or reaffirm your values, assess how well you are living these three common coaching values: integrity, humility, and caring.

A Foundation of Values

When we built our current home, we spent years plan-ning and designing every aspect and detail of the house. Throughout the long but worthwhile process, we discov-ered the criticality of a good foundation. Once our builder poured the foundation, we were committed to a certain floor plan and the way the house would flow. The foun-dation would set the stage for everything else we would build, and even how we would ultimately interact within the house. We chose to take extra measures to ensure we had a solid foundation, knowing that any movement could cause cracks in the future that would be difficult and expensive to repair.

Regardless of the quality of the framing and finish outside, a house—or any building, for that matter—is only as strong as its foundation. The Leaning Tower of Pisa in Italy, for example, leans about 17 feet because it was built on an inadequate foundation—a mere three meters, set in weak, unstable subsoil. Foundation problems can be difficult to detect, and our tendency is to fix the "symptom" rather than determine the root cause. We see a crack in a floor tile, so we replace the tile. A bedroom door doesn't swing quite right, so we adjust the hinges. A window doesn't close flush, so we caulk the bottom to seal the gap. But problems will continue to appear until we fix the real issue—the foundation.

Building a team, like building a house, starts with a solid foundation. A team's foundation is its values. Inspiring coaches know they must first pour a strong foundation of values before they can build a house to lead in. Once the values are set, they determine how the team will make decision and interact with one another. A strong foundation helps prevent problems in the team

> *The foundation stones for a balanced success are honesty, character, integrity, faith, love, and loyalty.*
>
> **—ZIG ZIGLAR**
> Author, Salesman, and Motivational Speaker

and ensures smooth interactions, sound decisions, and predictable results.

Just as in a home, we often tend to fix the symptoms rather than determine and fix the root cause of our team's issues. If you find yourself repeatedly dealing with the same issues on your team, they are likely symptoms of an underlying crack in your foundational values. For instance, you might observe an increase in product errors coming from your team, so you provide additional training and more detailed work procedures to reduce the error rate. However, if the root of the problem exists in your foundational values—perhaps a lack of mutual trust among team members—you can tinker all day with your team's work processes without improving results. Similarly, what looks like a minor blip in employee turnover could indicate a deeper problem of a disconnect between your values and your actions.

Your team is only as strong as the foundational values upon which it is built. Take the time to communicate your personal and team values again and again to your team. And most importantly, make the commitment to live and lead by them. Lee recalls the first time he expressed his leadership values to a team. He called them "Lee's 3 F's": *Focused, Fair,* and *Fun.* These leadership values formed the foundation for the behaviors he expected from his team and what they could expect from him.

We have helped many clients articulate their personal values to crystalize their coaching identity and their team values in order to facilitate communication of expectations. Below is sample output from an exercise we facilitate with clients to convert their values into behaviors they expect from their teams and behaviors their teams can expect from them.

COACHING VALUES	WHAT YOU CAN EXPECT FROM ME . . .	WHAT I CAN EXPECT FROM YOU . . .
Questions lead to quality	• I will answer any questions you have without judgment. • I will ask lots of questions to understand and test your thinking. • I will provide frequent feedback to quicken your pathway to quality output. • You will be my priority, so I will not be a bottleneck in your decision making.	Your work product reflects you! So: • Ask questions early and often. • Use your teammates to double-check your thinking and your work before presenting it. • Continuously learn by reading, studying, and watching others. We must always be changing and learning to deliver great quality.
Direct, respectful communication	• I will be honest because you deserve it and quality work requires it. • I will be direct because we do not have the time to be otherwise. • I will praise your performance in public and critique your performance in private.	• Tell me what is on your mind. That is the only way I can help you or change myself. • Respect others by addressing any concerns directly with them in the appropriate forum (if it is personal, do it in private).
Focus on the positive	• I will focus on the positive during our successes *and* during our challenges. • There will always be room for improvement, but there are also always good things happening and good opportunities ahead. I will recognize both.	• Look for the positive in any situation and stay focused on it in good times and in bad times. • Assume the best intent of others, even if what they are doing frustrates you.

COACHING VALUES	WHAT YOU CAN EXPECT FROM ME . . .	WHAT I CAN EXPECT FROM YOU . . .
Collaboration	• We are better tighter, so I will consistently ask for your ideas to improve the way we work and our work output. • I will speak like I am right, but I will listen like I am wrong. This will help me remain open to new ideas.	• Wild ideas are acceptable and expected. I also expect you to piggyback on my wild ideas. • Quantity of ideas versus quality of ideas will create a culture of innovation, so implement two new ideas each month, even if they are very small.
Accountability	• I will do what I say. • If something changes, I will give you a heads-up as soon as I am aware of the change. • I will set clear expectations up front to reduce ambiguity and increase your chances of meeting expectations.	• Do what you say. • Before you commit to a deadline (when work is due), assess your timeline (when works gets done). • Present a well-thought-out solution when you present a problem.

Values-Based Decisions

The power of choice is one of the greatest gifts we are given. In fact, it is so important that the privilege of choice is removed from prison inmates as a form of punishment. Although you make many choices every hour of the day, you rarely make neutral choices. Each choice has a positive or negative consequence at some level. Your decisions directly influence how you spend your precious resources—time, money and energy. How you spend your precious resources is a direct reflection of your values.

Benjamin Franklin addressed values-based decisions when he said, "We stand at the crossroads, each minute, each hour, each day, making choices. We choose the thoughts we allow ourselves to think, the passions we allow ourselves to feel, and the actions we allow ourselves to perform. Each choice is made in the context of whatever value systems we have selected to govern our lives. In selecting that value system, we are in a very real way, making the most important choice we will ever make . . . ."

> *It is not the beauty of a building you should look at; it's the construction of the foundation that will stand the test of time.*
>
> **—DAVID ALLAN COE**
> American Singer and Songwriter

If you don't use your values to make decisions and guide your actions, then why have them? If *you* do not value your values, no one else will. Your decisions directly influence how you spend your precious resources—time, money, and energy. How you spend your precious resources is a direct reflection of your values. A look at your calendar and your expense budget gives an accurate glimpse into what you value.

Making values-based decisions is not a once-in-awhile thing; it's a daily action. For example, you might say that your priorities for how you spend your time might be team members first, customers second, and upper management third. With that value to guide you, it becomes easier to say "yes" to spending your time with your higher-priority constituents and occasionally say "no" to requests from lower-priority constituents.

Saying "no" does not just mean saying it to other people. Inspiring coaches often say "no" to themselves. When we base our decisions on our values, we are willing to sacrifice today by saying "no" to something that might be fun or tempting, in order to achieve tomorrow's rewards of realizing our vision for a team, project, task, coaching interaction, etc.

Making values-based decisions removes much of the stress and pressure of making decisions "in the moment." When you hold your options or choices up to the mirror of your values, the right choice quickly becomes obvious. Aligning decisions with your values also ensures clear thinking about the consequences of those decisions—good or bad. In other words, consider today what the results of your action/decision will feel like in five hours, five days, and five years.

Select only a few core values, but live and lead by them unwaveringly, particularly when they are tough to stand by. Untested values are not as deeply held as tested values. The best way to test values is to apply them every day with each decision and interaction. So, as you are faced with decisions, use your values to help you determine what to do. Making values-based decisions sends a strong message to your team about the character of your leadership.

> *When your values are clear to you, making decisions becomes easier.*
>
> **—ROY E. DISNEY**
> Sr. Executive, Walt
> Disney Co.

CHAPTER 4

Know Your Emotions

*When dealing with people, remember
you are not dealing with creatures of logic,
but with creatures of emotion.*

—DALE CARNEGIE
SALES AND SELF-IMPROVEMENT GURU

nspiring coaches master their emotions and deal with them effectively. As a result, they are able to keep the main objective in mind and communicate their goal without getting caught up in their emotions. They move from being emotional to being emotionally intelligent.

"A leader's emotions are highly contagious," writes Annie McKee, a senior fellow at the University of

Pennsylvania Graduate School of Education and author of *How to Be Happy at Work,* in a blog on *Harvard Business Review.* So, you want to "manage your feelings accordingly to create the kind of environment where people can work together to make decisions and get things done."[1]

Controlling your emotions does not mean being emotionless. In fact, most people like and appreciate emotion as long as it is appropriate and constructive. Mastering your emotions enables you to intentionally elevate or calm your own and others' emotions to achieve a desired outcome. People will mirror your emotions. That's why discussions can easily become heated and counterproductive; each party matches and escalates the level of emotion. It's a lose-lose situation.

As the leader and coach, when you are aware of your emotions and keep an eye on the outcome instead of needing to be right, you can de-escalate the emotional tone of the conversation and enable clearer heads to work toward the desired outcome. It's a win-win. The mutual goal is more likely achieved and the relationship is enhanced instead of damaged.

You can intentionally manage your emotions to motivate, inspire, and encourage your team members as appropriate. Let's find out how.

Express Yourself

James Pennebaker, a professor at the University at Texas, has spent 40 years researching the link between writing and processing emotions. In studies, he has divided people into two groups, asking some to jot down emotionally charged experiences, and others to write about whatever daily occurrence popped into their mind. Both groups were tasked with writing for about 20 minutes, three days in a row.[2]

Pennebaker found that the people who wrote about their emotionally charged episodes experienced the most improvement in their physical well-being. They had lower blood pressure, better immunity, and visited the doctor less frequently. They were also less depressed, generally happier, and less anxious.

Unexpressed emotions do not go away. They eventually rear their heads in uglier ways. Journaling is a good way to delve into your feelings and gain a new perspective on your emotions. Knowing your own emotional triggers is key to constructively controlling your emotions. If someone does or says something that rubs you the wrong way, how will you avoid reacting in a way that prevents you from achieving your goal? When

> *I write because I don't know what I think (or feel) until I read what I say.*
>
> **—FLANNERY O'CONNOR**
> American writer and essayist

you learn to recognize your emotions and triggers, you can craft a plan to respond to the task at hand more deliberately. Rather than getting caught up in your emotions or bottling them up, you'll be able to act in a way that better serves you and your team.

Here are three proven steps to help you express and understand your emotions:

- **First, write your thoughts in a journal.** Writing is more visceral and tied to your emotions than typing, so this is one time you want to go old school and write down your thoughts. Be consistent, so a daily habit is daily is best. Start small with just a few minutes each morning while you still control your time.
- **Second, write whatever comes to mind.** Do not filter your thoughts or emotions. Consider a trigger question if it helps stimulate your thinking like: How am I feeling about my coaching? What deserves my best attention right now? What is the most interesting initiative I've heard about this week that is outside of my industry? What energized me the most this week? or What drained me the most?
- **Third, keep it to yourself.** You might choose to act on the insights you gain from your journaling, but your raw, written thoughts and emotions are for you only. Your emotions become clearer on the journey between your mind and your pen.

Emotions and Empathy

Inspiring coaches are savvy enough to know when it's time to address an issue. They read other people and understand the nuances of a situation. In other words, they have emotional intelligence.

One of the cornerstones of emotional intelligence is empathy. According to Sara D. Hodges and Michael W. Myers in the *Encyclopedia of Social Psychology*, "Empathy is often defined as understanding another person's experience by imagining oneself in that other person's situation. One understands the other person's experience as if it were being experienced by the self, but without the self actually experiencing it."[3]

So, why is empathy important? It helps you more genuinely connect with your team. It also helps you determine the right time and creates the appropriate context to provide constructive coaching. In being able to empathize, you're not taking on another person's problems. You're considering how they feel so you can convey information in a way that is sure to resonate with them.

When you take time to understand where someone is coming from, even when you're going through a tough time yourself, it will be easier to come up with a plan that improves the dynamic. Rather than react in a way that makes the situation worse, you'll convey the

> *When you show deep empathy toward others, their defensive energy goes down, and positive energy replaces it. That's when you can get more creative in solving problems.*
>
> **—STEPHEN COVEY**
> Author, *The 7 Habits of Highly Effective People*

appropriate feelings, which your team members may mirror or exhibit themselves.

Of course, being empathetic takes practice. It doesn't come overnight. To be empathetic, you need to be open and willing to recognize the feelings of others. You can bolster your empathy in other ways, too, from casting aside stereotypes and snap judgments to simply asking someone how their day is going.

As social philosopher and writer Roman Krznaric explains in his book, *Empathy: Why It Matters, and How to Get It*, perhaps the greatest thing you can do to be more empathetic is to simply listen.[4] Give people the chance to explain where they're coming from and consider repeating back what they've said to show that you've understood.

"Response-ability"

Think of the last time you were in deep thought about your plans for the evening while driving home from work.

As you pull into your driveway you wonder to yourself, "How did I get home?" The car seemed to practically drive itself home. Driving is a relatively complex task, requiring many choices along the way: turn right, turn left, slow down, stop, and change lanes. Still, driving home can be successfully performed almost subconsciously. Now, consider the multitude of much smaller choices we make each day that we don't really think about: waking up, brushing our teeth, saying "good morning" to a colleague, eating our lunch, performing a repetitive job duty, and so on. Subconscious actions are useful most of the time, but we must also consciously choose our emotions to control our reactions.

Here is a scenario that plays out daily in organizations everywhere. Cathy is a leader and coach. Emily is on her team. For the second time in a row, Emily was late turning in her sales status report that is due the last Friday of the month at four o'clock. This results in her leader, Cathy, having to present incomplete or inaccurate sales projections to her vice president at the monthly sales meeting. Cathy's blood is starting to boil because this chips away at her personal credibility with her leader. This is no time for an e-mail, so Cathy jumps out of her office chair and starts marching down to Emily's desk.

Here is a *reaction* to this situation: "Not again, Emily! This is *not* that hard to do. Do you realize the situation you are putting me in? What's your problem?"

Here is a *response* to this event: "Emily, it is important for the company to communicate accurate sales forecasts to our investors, so that's why I need your sales status report no later than four o'clock the last Friday of the month. This is the second month in a row you missed the deadline. I am pretty frustrated right now, so I would like to meet Monday and I want you to tell me what needs to change in order for you to consistently meet this deadline moving forward."

Which one leads to better relationships and better sustained results—a reaction or a response? When you *react*, you make a purely emotional and subconscious decision. Because of how your experiences and prior choices have programmed your subconscious mind, your reactions often do not help you achieve the best results or maintain positive relationships. On the other hand, when you *respond* to a situation, you check your emotions first. You make a constructive and conscious decision. That's why there are Emergency Response Teams and not Emergency Reaction Teams.

Your ability to choose whether to react or respond is a gift. No matter what today's "it's not my fault" culture encourages, you are ultimately responsible for your own choices. In fact, we like to write the word "responsibility" as *response–ability*. As humans, we have the unique ability to respond. It is a choice we make, although too often it's a subconscious rather than conscious choice:

- When you simply *react*, your emotional instinct is in control, with little thought of the long-range consequences.
- When you *respond*, your brain is fully engaged, and your self-awareness is high. You have the long-term consequences in mind.

Let's say you're coaching Austin, a team leader, on asking more questions to engage the team instead of giving them the answer. Austin gets defensive and even accusatory toward you since he sees himself as very engaging and you have exposed one of his blind spots. You could easily react to prove you're right, which would elevate the emotional tenor of the discussion.

Alternatively, with awareness of your own emotions, you realize that the issue is not Austin's defensiveness, what he said to you, or how his comment made you feel. You simply pointed out a blind spot, and Austin reacted. Your goal is to achieve a positive outcome so you reassure Austin of his signature strengths and remind him of your goal for this discussion—to elevate his leadership. You also remind him that he needs to be a willing participant and be open to your coaching to elevate his game.

You have risen above an emotional reaction and responded with respect, calmness, and firmness. Choosing to respond instead of reacting increases predictability for others and reduces their stress when they interact with us.

Master Your Responses

We all experience plenty of negative situations and people. The key is to be prepared to consciously respond to these negative inputs. One way to help keep your emotions in balance regardless of the circumstances is to use the simple 5 × 5 Rule: *If it won't matter in five years don't spend more than five minutes being upset by it.*

Despite our intentions, we sometimes find ourselves in the midst of a subconscious negative reaction. If you find yourself having a negative reaction, say "STOP!" out loud, and replace it with a positive response. Saying "STOP!" out loud is important so that you can actually hear yourself controlling your own emotions and responses. Let's see how it works. Here is an example from Lee. (Trust us, we both have plenty of other stories that would not serve as positive examples for this section!)

I was running late for a 5:55 p.m. flight to give a speech. I parked my car in the expensive infield parking lot to save time. I bolted through the parking lot and sprinted into the terminal. Then, I came to a complete halt at the security check point. I finally got through security with only 10 minutes to departure time. I sped up to a slow sprint as I weaved my way through people and courtesy carts. I passed my favorite frozen yogurt stand (oh, the price of running late!) and burst up to the gate to be greeted by a sign reading, "Flight 619 to Vail departs 8:55 p.m." Delayed three hours?!

I felt my blood pressure rising and a desire to react to the nearest gate agent. Fortunately, I caught myself and literally said, "STOP!" (Okay, it was not quite that loud, but certainly audible enough to turn a few curious heads.) But, that's all I needed to prevent an unproductive reaction. Instead, I chose to respond. I decided I would spend the time catching up on the day's news, reading a chapter of a book I had brought along, and even writing a little of the book you are reading now. Then, I would make a few phones calls to reconnect with some friends and check in with my kids. I could feel my blood pressure dropping.

> **The more aware we are, the less likely any trigger, even in the most mundane circumstances, will prompt hasty unthinking behavior that leads to undesirable consequences.**
>
> **—DR. MARSHALL GOLDSMITH**
> Author, *Triggers: Creating Behavior That Lasts—Becoming the Person You Want to Be*

As I found a seat and settled in, I saw in my periphery a well-dressed man doing the same high-speed approach to the gate. He threw his backpack on the counter and said, "Did the plane leave yet?" The agent pointed to the sign behind her and said, "No, I am sorry, sir. It has been delayed." He reacted by barking out,

"I am a Platinum level member in your frequent flier program! Let me talk to your supervisor!" He proceeded to berate the supervisor, make ridiculous demands, make calls on his cell phone, and treated the people on the other end of the calls rudely. His tantrum went on and on. I lost interest once he started repeating his routine. Well, guess what time the plane left? Right, 8:55 p.m., still three hours late. His reaction did nothing to improve the end result, but it certainly damaged some relationships.

The facts of both our situations were the same, but this man boarded the plane still fuming. I'm glad that I did not have to sit next to him! Not only was he late, but he had also spent three hours unproductively. I had a bounce in my step because I chose to do some writing, read a bit, and catch up with people who were important to me. The bottom line was that I chose to manage my response and was getting the best of myself, while this gentleman was letting the situation get the best of him.

> **A gentle response defuses anger, but a sharp tongue kindles a temper-fire.**
>
> **—PROVERBS 15:1**

Knowing and mastering your emotions empowers and equips you to be a more confident person, a more empathetic friend person, a more relatable leader, and of course, a more inspiring coach.

Positive Mindset Summary

1. Know Your Thoughts

- ✓ Maintain a positive thought life by controlling input from media, others, and you.
- ✓ Choose to look for positive performance and traits; that's what your mind's eye will see.
- ✓ Seek unfiltered truth about your coaching from your team to prevent blind spots.
- ✓ Create "mental space" for self-reflection and planning.

2. Know Your Purpose

- ✓ Focus on how many people you serve versus how many people serve you.
- ✓ Connect with your team by finding common ground.
- ✓ Facilitate connections amongst team members to boost engagement and productivity.
- ✓ Invest in others to build future leaders and better lives for themselves.

3. Know Your Values

✓ Pour a strong foundation of values on which to build a winning team.

✓ Incorporate common values for inspiring coaches: integrity, humility, and caring.

✓ Convert your values into observable behaviors to bring them to life.

✓ Your values are reflected in your daily decisions, so view your calendar and your budget as reflections of your values.

4. Know Your Emotions

✓ Keep a private journal to help you know and manage your emotions.

✓ Demonstrate empathy to more effectively navigate challenging coaching discussions.

✓ Respond (versus react) to situations by checking your emotions first so you can make the best decisions for your team.

✓ Master your emotions with the 5 × 5 Rule: If it won't matter in five years don't spend more than five minutes being upset by it.

71

TAKING ACTION

Positive Coaching Mindset

1. What am I doing today to better understand myself and my impact on others?

_____

_____

_____

2. Who can I better serve?

_____

_____

_____

3. What are my personal values? How do they translate into my coaching behaviors?

_____

_____

_____

4. What is the biggest trigger that throws me off my emotional balance? How can I better anticipate and manage that trigger?

_____

_____

_____

PART II

Positive Coaching Habits

Coaches are sculptors.
They might not shape marble,
but they shape something much
more precious: people's lives.

—LEE J. COLAN

Your coaching mindset will set the limits for the level of impact your coaching habits will have on your team's performance. A positive coaching mindset enables you to authentically and effectively apply the coaching habits and reap the ultimate benefit—winning results and relationships. On the other hand, with a negative coaching mindset your coaching habits will inhibit your ability to inspire your team and yield less than optimal results.

There are five positive coaching habits. When they are applied with a positive coaching mindset, you will predictably inspire winning results and relationships. These five habits give your team the biggest boost if applied in sequence, but you should still use your knowledge of each team member to determine when to accelerate through or spend more time on a specific habit. The root meaning of the verb "to coach" means to bring a person from where he or she is to where he or she wants to be. The inspiring coach focuses more on developing a person's natural gifts so each team member can realize his or her potential while shoring up weaknesses to help each team member master his or her job.

Consider the role of a football coach. He sets clear expectations for his team with a game plan to win. He asks players if they have any questions to ensure they are clear about their respective roles on the team. He also asks them questions like, "How can you improve your performance or overcome a certain obstacle?" Then during the game, he involves them in changing the game plan, if necessary, based on what they are seeing on the field. The coach also observes and measures each player's performance (e.g., number of tackles, yards gained, etc.). Finally, the coach gives constructive feedback and recognition so his players can elevate their performance in the next game.

These are the five positive habits that inspiring coaches in business practice to build winning teams:

1. **Inspiring coaches *explain expectations*.** They take the time to ensure alignment with their teams before moving forward.

2. **Inspiring coaches *ask questions*.** A leader asks to clarify a problem or for ideas and suggestions. Asking questions ignites employee engagement.

3. **Inspiring coaches *involve team members*** in creating solutions to improve their work. This enlists ownership because people are committed to things they help create.

4. **Inspiring coaches *measure results*** diligently to boost team accountability.

5. **Inspiring coaches *appreciate people*.** This builds commitment to sustaining and improving results.

Using each of these habits in concert elevates team performance.

The 5 Positive Coaching Habits

Habit	**Result**
1 EXPLAIN Expectations	**Alignment**
2 ASK Questions	**Engagement**
3 INVOLVE Team	**Ownership**
4 MEASURE Results	**Accountability**
5 APPRECIATE People	**Commitment**

The left side of this model shows five positive coaching habits that inspire winning results and relationships. This is the *side of choice*. Each day, coaches choose whether to take these actions. Their choices influence the right side of this model—the *results*. If you choose your habits, then you must take responsibility for your results. You are responsible for the choices you make and for the results you ultimately achieve. If you choose *not* to build these coaching habits, you must accept these predictable outcomes:

- Instead of Alignment, you get Confusion
- Instead of Engagement, you get Disengagement
- Instead of Ownership, you get Entitlement
- Instead of Accountability, you get Blame
- Instead of Commitment, you get Compliance

These positive coaching habits are based on natural human dynamics and needs. That's why it does not look like rocket science and seems so simple. That's also why these habits work across generations, industries, and cultures; they meet universal human needs in the workplace. It is easy for one thing or another to get in the way of these habits, but if you say "yes" to those things, you are saying "no" to winning results and relationships. Positive coaching is not a "salt and pepper" practice. You cannot sprinkle on a little *explaining* here and *appreciation* there and expect winning results or relationships. You must perform these habits consistently. If world-class athletes need a coach every day, why wouldn't your team?

Each day you're making a choice about your team's alignment, engagement, ownership, accountability, and commitment. Let's see how a team leader, Lexi, and an employee, Cameron, progress through the five positive coaching habits:

> **Lexi:** "Hey, Cameron. I'm glad I bumped into you. I wanted to talk to you about something. We really need to improve our response time on special orders. If we do, we will create a positive ripple effect with our core customer, which will drive sales, and that's good for all of us." *(Lexi is explaining expectations and consequences.)*
>
> **Cameron:** "OK, I understand." *(Cameron is simply observing.)*
>
> **Lexi:** "You're on the front lines with this issue. Why do you think our response time has increased lately?" *(Lexi is asking questions.)*
>
> **Cameron:** "Well, the new system migration has had its bumps. But I think the bigger issue is that we weren't prepared for the recent promotional campaign for our VIP customers. Our call volume from VIPs has increased by 80 percent for special orders over the same period last quarter."
> *(Cameron is becoming engaged.)*

Lexi: "We need to discuss your ideas on how we can get back on track. Our response time has a direct impact on our bottom line, so I'll give you whatever support you need to take care of this." *(Lexi is involving Cameron.)*

Cameron: "That sounds great. Let me get some input from my team and send you some recommendations before our meeting. I'm confident we can identify a good solution and implement it quickly." *(Now Cameron is owning the solution.)*

Lexi: *(After they meet.)* "I like your recommendations, Cameron. Let's measure the key metrics you identified each week for the next month and touch base to see if we need to tweak anything." *(Lexi is observing performance and providing feedback along the way.)*

Cameron: *(next month)* "Looks like we're in good shape. Our response time has gone down each week, and we have been at our target of 20 percent reduction in response time for the past two weeks. How about if I just keep an eye on things now and send you a quick scorecard each month to ensure we sustain the changes?" *(Cameron is taking accountability for the results.)*

Lexi: "That sounds great, Cameron. I am really impressed with how you took control of this challenge, involved your team and executed the solution. I really appreciate your efforts. Well done!" *(Lexi is appreciating Cameron and his performance.)*

Since Lexi applied the five positive coaching habits, Cameron is feeling a sense of personal commitment to his job and to his coach. Plus, he is motivated to deliver results so he can be reinforced by his coach again, because it feels good. Everyone likes to be reinforced for their performance.

Inspiring coaches integrate the positive coaching habits into their daily interactions, realizing it is the best formula for winning. Let's take a closer look at each of the five positive coaching habits and how they can help you inspire winning results and relationships for your team.

> *A coach is someone who tells you what you don't want to hear, who has you see what you don't want to see, so you can be who you always knew you could be.*
>
> **—TOM LANDRY**
> Hall of Fame Football Coach, Dallas Cowboys

CHAPTER 5

Positive Coaching Habit #1:

EXPLAIN Expectations to Gain Alignment

Unclear expectations lead to unclear destinations.

—LEE J. COLAN

Many of today's leadership practices are rooted in historical military testing, application, and refinement. But what can business leaders gain from current-day military, specifically Navy, leadership practices that have been honed for years and now are used with today's more complex, competitive leadership environment? A lot!

The next time you hear a business leader complain about "the new generation worker" and how they cannot motivate them and how they take no initiative, consider this:

Lee, coauthor of this book, had the privilege of spending a weekend aboard the USS *Abraham Lincoln,* about 100 miles offshore as it prepared for a deployment. This aircraft carrier is the proud flagship of the Navy's fleet and is a floating city. Over 5,000 sailors live and work on it. They perform the most complex flight operations in the most tumultuous conditions, day and night, with *zero degrees of freedom.* The cost of error is tens of millions of dollars in damaged Navy assets or even loss of life. No *Top Gun* movie scene here. This is the real-life danger zone!

This type of environment demands nothing less than fully synchronized teamwork, passionate selflessness, relentless effort, and consistent execution. All this is delivered by sailors with an average age of 20 years old. So, this peak level of performance is achieved with thousands of 18- and 19-year-olds, most of whom did not have a clear direction after graduating high school, let alone have an MBA. It is mind-boggling when we couch this against clients who are frustrated with their highly educated team's performance while they are working in nicely appointed, air-conditioned, land-based offices. At the core of this level of Naval performance is crystal-clear expectations.

At the most basic level, the job of a coach is to equip team members with knowledge and tools to be successful. A leader is only successful if his or her team is successful. That includes educating team members on organizational systems like budgeting, goal setting, and authority levels for spending and training. The leader must also educate his or her team on informal "learning the ropes" things like company culture norms during working hours, lunchtime, meetings etiquette, attire, how presentations are made, key people to keep in the loop, and how decisions are really made, regardless of what the policy states. Equipping your team by explaining these aspects of the job is not a one-time thing you check off your leadership list. Inspiring coaches continually explain, educate, and equip their team with tips, tools, training, and insights.

Just like winning a sports game starts at the beginning with good practice, winning in business starts at the beginning of the performance process. If you wait until the end, then you are simply imposing consequences rather than inspiring positive performance. That's why aligning on expectations is a good predictor of winning business results. Expectation gaps lead to execution gaps. The large majority of performance frustrations stem from not communicating clear expectations up front. Therefore, the coaching key is to front-end-load clarity. You and your team should be able to easily align on the answer to this question: "How will I know if I have met expectations?" We cannot rely on others' perceptions of our expectations. The imperfect nature of human communication requires us to be more specific than we think we need to be. Lack of clear expectations is the most common reason for performance problems. There is not really a close second. Gaining alignment through clear expectations is job No. 1 for inspiring coaches.

The Fundamental Four Questions

To gain alignment, explain your answers to the following Fundamental Four Questions. These are questions that every employee asks, regardless of whether you hear them:

1. Where are we going? (*Goals*)
2. What are we doing to get there? (*Plans*)
3. How can I contribute? (*Roles*)
4. What's in it for me? (*Rewards*)

Like any aspect of leadership, gaining alignment does not just happen. It must be intentional. Our late friend and inspiring coach Ron Rossetti liked to say, "Awesomeness is never accidental." Our clients who paint a clear picture for their teams are intentional about answering the Fundamental Four Questions. They use the questions as a checklist to ensure that the content of significant company communications addresses each question. The alignment in their organizations is notably greater and their results are notably better. Answering the Fundamental Four Questions creates a bridge that connects today's tasks to the broader team purpose.

Inspiring coaches help their teams see and understand the longer-term, downstream impact of their personal performance on team results, on the organization, on customers, on shareholders, and ultimately on themselves (What's in it for me?). When employees see how their actions help or hinder others, it aligns their performance with clear consequences. The personal impact to an employee might include opportunities for promotions, development, exposure to executives, public recognition, expanded responsibilities, flexibility in the job, oversight of others, ownership of projects, and/or financial rewards.

In addition to *formal* communication, explain expectations for your team with each *informal* communication. For example, you can pop into their workspace or call remote team members to see how they are doing. With today's information-overloaded workplace, it can be challenging to decide what to communicate to employees and what to withhold. It's easy to say (usually to yourself), "They don't really need to know all that," or, "My team won't really understand," or, "I don't think they can handle that news right now." Be cautious because those who *under*estimate the intelligence of others tend to *over*estimate their own.

When employees don't get the necessary information to perform their jobs, including the answers to the Fundamental Four Questions, they tend to "fill in the blanks" with their own assumptions, and their assumptions are often worst-case scenarios. This is not necessarily a reflection on the leader. It's our natural human insecurity. We often assume the worst in the absence of evidence to the contrary. Lack of information and unanswered questions can start the silence spiral:

> Silence leads to doubt;
>> Doubt leads to fear;
>>> Fear leads to panic;
>>>> Panic leads to worst-case thinking.

The silence spiral undermines trust and puts a damper on passion. It can take five minutes or five weeks to play out, but in most cases, it happens more rapidly than we would imagine. A closed office door, a vague reply to an honest question, an unreciprocated greeting as you pass in the hallway, or a canceled one-on-one meeting can all trigger the silence spiral.

Prevent the silence spiral by proactively explaining expectations. Nothing compares to hearing the facts directly from the boss. For example, if you learn about a new project or change that won't affect your team for a few months, go ahead and give them a heads-up now. They can start preparing, or at minimum, they won't be caught off guard or be inclined to listen to and perpetuate rumors. Inspiring coaches realize they are not really protecting their teams by keeping them in the dark. Employees will either find out on their own or may make assumptions that are worse than reality. More importantly, silence chips away at trust and your leadership credibility. So, use every interaction, meeting, and communication to explain expectations.

The 3 *W's*—*What, Who,* and *When*

Inspiring coaches help their teams by clearly and specifically defining the actions, timing, and results they expect from others and from themselves. For each member of your team, make certain you communicate the 3 *W's*— *What, Who,* and *When*.

WHAT	WHO	WHEN	STATUS/COMMENTS
1.			
2.			
3.			

We use this simple format with our coaching clients to help them drive millions of dollars in improvement. The power is in its simplicity. To ensure clear expectations when using the 3W form, identify only one "Who" per action. This will avoid "two-headed monsters" since a "We" is unowned and undone. This simple 3W form is even more powerful when you carry it with you as a mental template to bring closure to daily conversations and interactions. We each bring our own perceptions, experiences, and assumptions to every interaction, so the chance that we will be in sync after a discussion is quite low. Since human communication is much more art than science, clarifying the 3 W's after even short conversations helps identify perception gaps and ensure both parties are aligned on respective actions.

Although aligning on clear expectations can be tedious, if you take the necessary time to do it, you will end up spending less time dealing with performance problems and more time executing your plan. A broad and persuasive series of studies confirms that specificity of goals dramatically increases the likelihood of success. For example, in one study, participants were asked to write a report on how they spent Christmas Eve, and then to write that report within two days after Christmas Eve. Half of the participants were required to specify when and where within those two days they intended to write the report. The other half was not required to give specifics. Among those who had to provide specifics, 71 percent handed the reports in on time. Only 32 percent of the second group did so.[1]

Explain the Fourth *W—Why*

To ensure alignment, inspiring coaches do not shy away from discussions of consequences, but they use a broad definition of consequences. We tend to think of consequences in terms of the short-term, immediate impact of our performance (positive or negative). That's the easy part of defining specific consequences. But it still leaves a lot to the imagination. As the Circle of Consequences below illustrates, you need to help employees see and understand the longer-term, downstream impact of their performance on team results, on the organization, on customers, on shareholders, and ultimately on themselves. This helps you align with your team by explaining the fourth *W—Why*.

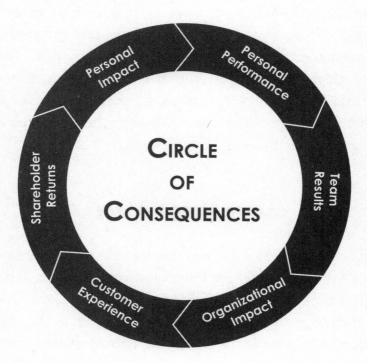

When employees see how their actions help or hinder each of their various constituents, the personal consequences of their performance become self-evident. External performance is ultimately a reflection of internal commitment. The personal impact to an employee might include opportunities for more (or fewer if the performance is substandard) promotions, development opportunities, exposure to executives, public recognition, responsibilities, flexibility in the job, oversight of others, ownership of projects, and/or financial rewards. It is fair and appropriate to bring personal performance full circle back to these consequences. Our clients have found it useful to follow the Circle of Consequences with respect to their own leadership behavior, particularly when they face tough situations. It illuminates the impact of their actions (or lack thereof) on various constituents and usually moves them from complying with the task to being committed to it.

Learn Along the Way

Let's say you're taking a road trip for your family summer vacation. You're going to your favorite beach that is a 1,000-mile drive. You're aligned on the destination. Even though the driver knows the destination, he or she must still check in with the navigator (coach) at each turn, merge and exit on the highway to ensure you stay on course. The same is true when you coach a team member. It is necessary, but not sufficient, to explain expectations up front. To help him or her win and arrive at the right destination, several course corrections, or at least course confirmations, might be required along the journey. This means debriefing interactions, meetings, presentations, etc. with the employee. Even if they are someone else's interactions, meetings, and presentations, it helps the employee learn what should and should not be done to be successful by observing others. Use every opportunity as a chance to align on expectations and coach for future success. Don't confine your mid-course feedback to direc-

> *People can't live up to the expectations they don't know have been set for them.*
>
> **—RORY VADEN**
> Author, *Take the Stairs*

tions only. Discuss how the driver (employee) is driving—the manner of performance. Is he or she staying in the lane (remaining focused on the task), checking blind spots (seeking feedback from others), and going the right speed (maintaining a sense of urgency)? Explaining expectations is not a one-time coaching event. Inspiring coaches see it as a continuous cycle of explain-observe-coach-adjust-align. It's a cycle of victory.

POSITIVE COACHING HABIT SUMMARY

 EXPLAIN Expectations

- Answer the Fundamental Four Questions (goals, plans, roles, and rewards).
- Align on the 3 W's—*What, Who,* and *When*.
- Explain the fourth W—*Why,* using the Circle of Consequences.
- Learn along the way: debrief after interactions, meetings, presentations, milestones.

> 66 *We must explain the game plan to win the game.* 99
>
> —LEE J. COLAN

TAKING ACTION

EXPLAIN Expectations to Gain Alignment

1. How can I intentionally share my team's goals, plans, roles, and rewards (i.e., answer the Fundamental Four Questions) in my daily interactions and meetings?

_____

_____

_____

_____

_____

_____

_____

2. How can I institutionalize the use of the 3 _W_'s (_What, Who_, and _When_) as a follow-up to our meetings?

_____

_____

_____

_____

_____

_____

_____

CHAPTER 6

Positive Coaching Habit #2:

ASK Questions to Ignite Engagement

*Questions are the golden keys
that unlock hearts and minds.*

—BOB TIEDE
AUTHOR, *GREAT LEADERS ASK QUESTIONS*

Explaining expectations is the first habit of inspiring coaches. But explaining is only a one-way process. To continue to inspire winning results and relationships, ask questions to initiate two-way communication and engage your team. Coaching is more about asking questions than it is about knowing the answers. Managers *tell* while coaches *ask*. Business schools don't teach courses on asking questions, so leaders rarely, if ever, study the art of questioning the way they would study financial reports. Additionally, most leadership training focuses on identifying problems and creating solutions, but inspiring coaches focus on asking the right questions to help their teams identify problems and create solutions. This skill better engages teams, and it also takes the pressure off the coach to know all the answers. When it comes to coaching, questions are really the answer. Asking questions is a long-established practice to demonstrate respect, diffuse tense situations, obtain buy-in, and make employees feel valued in a way that financial rewards cannot. Questions either expand or limit the solutions and creativity to seize opportunities and solve problems.

A few summers ago, we enjoyed a family trip to Greece. It is a land of boundless beauty and tremendous thinkers. While touring the Acropolis, our guide mentioned that while scheduling its restoration, time was built into each worker's day to spend time thinking! Imagine that happening almost anywhere else in the world, but since Greece's history is built upon the minds of the world's greatest thinkers it makes sense. One of those great thinkers is the Greek philosopher Socrates, who was born over 2,500 years ago. Today, Socrates is alive and well in any coach who inspires others to realize their potential. His Socratic method of questioning is a timely and timeless leadership tool for engaging teams and challenging thought processes. Asking questions is both selfless and self-serving. It demonstrates interest in your team while providing you with insights into their motivations, passions, challenges, assumptions, and aspirations. The next time you are tempted to tell your team what to do, take a lesson from Socrates and ask what they think first.

By simply asking questions, your employees will reveal challenges and opportunities that could potentially take you months or even years to identify. Asking questions and then really listening demonstrates personal respect and a genuine desire to engage and develop your team. Listen for the entire message your employee is communicating with his or her words, tone, posture, eyes, energy, hesitations, fluency, etc. Inspiring coaches listen at least 50 percent of the time. Andrew Levi, a client and excellent leader of numerous businesses, has done a tremendous amount of leading, presenting, pitching, directing, persuading, and explaining in his efforts to build winning cultures and businesses. When asked about the topic of listening, he directly replied, "He who talks the most loses."[1] Ask, be silent, and listen to engage your team.

Purposeful Questions

Plenty of books are filled with lists of questions. However, asking questions without a clear objective is like playing the question Lotto. Very occasionally you might get lucky and win, but most of the time you will come up empty-handed. That's a loss for you and for your team member. There is rarely a right answer to a wrong question.

There are four main reasons to ask questions: to understand, to assess, to innovate, and to motivate. It is important to know your objectives before you start asking. Within each objective, your question might focus on the person or the project/process. For example, if you want to understand your team's *projects* and *processes,* ask questions like:

- What's the goal?
- What's the plan?
- What are your options?

In addition, inspiring coaches ask questions to help understand their *people,* such as:

- In which areas would *you* like to grow?
- What do *you* love to do?
- What do *you* need to be at your very best?

Showing genuine interest in your employees as people is the foundation of a fully engaged team. Theodore Roosevelt summed it up nicely when he said, "People don't care how much you know until they know how much you care." If you need to motivate your people to action, you might ask:

- What needs to happen for this to succeed?
- What do *you* think the next steps should be?
- What's in it for *you* and the team if this is wildly successful?

Certain coaching questions work in almost any situation. These are some of our favorites that we have heard inspiring coaches ask:

- What do *you* think?
- Why do *you* think this is happening?
- What can we *start, stop, and keep* in order to improve our work?
- And what else? (Repeated as a prompt to obtain more details.)
- Is this your very best work? (Lee's mentor asks him this question.)

When coaching to improve performance, ask questions to identify the root cause of the performance problem. People initially respond with a symptom to the problem (We missed the project timeline because we were understaffed), but additional clarifying questions reveal the root cause (The team was not properly trained, and roles were not defined and documented).

The following table serves as a guide to keep your coaching questions purposeful:

Asking Purposeful Questions

UNDERSTAND To gain knowledge and solicit insights	ASSESS To determine options and make decisions
The Person • In which areas would you like to grow? • What do you love to do? • What do you need to be at your very best? • What would you like to be doing in three years? • How can we more fully utilize your skills? • What are you really passionate about? • What's your "why," your core motivation for working?	**The Person** • What would you change if you were in my position? • What's the most important thing you can accomplish today? • Which option makes the most sense to you? • What are the consequences of the choices? • What does your gut tell you? • What one thing could you improve to elevate your game?
The Project/Process • What's the goal? • What is your plan? • What are the alternative choices being considered? • What's the current situation? • What would you need to make this project succeed? • Who are the key players on your team? • Who are the stakeholders?	**The Project/Process** • What is your next step? • What conclusions have you reached so far? • What's the biggest risk? • What are the key factors in making this decision? • What is conflicting with your most important priorities? • How can we collect 80% of the data we need in the shortest time possible?

INNOVATE To generate ideas and improve methods	MOTIVATE To achieve a goal and implement a plan
The Person • What would you do if funds were unlimited? • What would you do differently if you had no fear of failing? • When do you feel the most creative? • Who do you brainstorm the best with? • What's one thing you would change today? • What do you think our business will look like in 10 years? **The Project/Process** • What if we looked at this from a totally different perspective? • How could we do this in half the time? • Who does this process better than anyone in the world? • Which steps do not add value to our customer? • What is one more alternative to consider?	**The Person** • What needs to happen for this to succeed? • What do you think the next steps should be? • What's in it for you and the team if this is wildly successful? • How can I best help or support you? • How can we maintain focus and excitement? • Do we have the right people in the right roles the ensure success? **The Project/Process** • What barriers do you need removed? • How will we know if we are successful? • What are the key milestones we must hit to stay on track? • What are a few quick wins we can achieve and celebrate? • What is the accountability process? • What's going well so far?

The Sound of Silence

Most people go to great lengths to avoid silence during conversations. They fill silence with anything, regardless of how meaningful (or meaningless). It is as if silence has its own gravitational force that pulls words from our mouths to prevent a single moment of silence. Of course, we have all experienced those three seconds of silence that felt like three minutes.

Inspiring coaches not only know the right questions to ask, but they also know how to patiently wait for an answer. They are comfortable with silence. If you're not comfortable with the silence, you will fill it with another question that leaves your original question unanswered and squelches engagement. After asking an employee a question, your patience creates power. Resist the gravitational pull to fill the void. Your silence creates accountability for a response. It's better to wait for a well-thought-out response than get a quick, half-baked reply.

Timelines versus Deadlines

We live in a world that trains us to meet deadlines, starting in grade school: Your paper is due May 15; college applications are due October 1; finish your community service hours by August 1; taxes are due April 15; the budget is due November 15; your annual goals are due January 15; your payment is due by February 1. Deadlines, deadlines, deadlines. Your team's inherent desire is to meet a deadline to please you, their leader; however, people typically fail to consider timelines before committing to deadlines. So, inspiring coaches focus on timelines (when work gets done) to meet deadlines (when work is due).

For example, say it's a Tuesday morning and you ask an employee: "Hey, Ryan, I need this market analysis finalized by Friday noon. It should only take a few hours to clean it up from the last draft you showed me. Can you please do that for me?" Ryan replies, "Sure, I'll take care of it!" Then Ryan goes back to his office, checks his calendar, and says to himself, "Oh bummer! I didn't realize I had all these commitments, day and night, and have no available time between now and Friday noon." At this point, the typical response for most people is to go into face-saving and avoidance modes. Ryan feels like he cannot go back on his word after he just so confidently told you he would take care of it. He also hopes that if he just avoids it you might forget to ask him for the analysis at noon on Friday. Yes, these responses sound irrational and even ridiculous, but they're very predictable human tendencies in the workplace. So, when Friday noon arrives you naturally expect the analysis from Ryan. By 1 p.m. you swing by his office to ask him where it is. Ryan's stomach sinks as he comes clean. You're frustrated because you, like any leader, hate surprises when it comes to missed deadlines. Ryan does not feel good about his performance and neither do you. It's a lose-lose situation, as the results are not delivered on time and the relationship credibility is damaged. This is a predictable scenario when you don't ask about your team member's timelines before he or she commits to a deadline.

Paul Spiegelman is the former CEO of The Beryl Companies and Chief Culture Officer of Stericycle. He has found a healthy balance between driving performance and the award-winning culture he has stewarded at his booming company. Spiegelman explains, "We don't like surprises. It's okay to give a leader a heads-up—that shows you are managing to timelines. But if you don't give a heads-up and you miss the deadline, then you are just managing deadlines."[2] Avoid surprises and improve alignment by negotiating timelines to determine deadlines your team members can meet.

Manage How You Ask

In an age when much more is being written than spoken, appreciation for the tone of the written word is being lost. For example, a typical cryptic text or e-mail relies on emojis to communicate a serious, sarcastic, or playful tone. Even the craftiest emoji user loses subtle intended meaning. When you're speaking, the words you stress can change the underlying meaning of a sentence.

Look at the following sentence: *I don't think he should lead the project.* This simple sentence can have many levels of meaning based on the word you stress. Consider the meaning of the following sentences with the stressed word in **bold**. Read each sentence aloud and stress the word in **bold**:

1. **Do** you think he should lead the project?
   MEANING: *Somebody else thinks he should lead the project.*

2. Do **you** think he should lead the project?
   MEANING: *What is your perspective?*

3. Do you **think** he should lead the project?
   MEANING: *Are you sure about your perspective?*

4. Do you think **he** should lead the project?
   MEANING: *Should somebody else lead the project?*

5. Do you think he **should** lead the project?
   MEANING: *Has he earned the chance to lead the project?*

6. Do you think he should **lead** the project?
   MEANING: *Can he handle the lead role?*

7. Do you think he should lead **the** project?
   MEANING: *Are you sure about this particular project?*

8. Do you think he should lead the **project**?
   MEANING: *Is he ready for a project lead role yet?*

As you can see, this simple eight-word sentence can be interpreted in eight different ways, resulting in unreliable written communication. Today's information-rich, time-poor world forces us to write and speak more specifically and clearly than ever. If you do not, you're rolling the dice. In the above illustration, you have just a one-in-eight, or 12.5 percent, chance that others will receive the same simple message you're sending. In addition, your tone and emphasis in communication create inference and judgment. So, when seeking to understand, use a neutral tone and equal emphasis of words to elicit an unfiltered and uninfluenced spoken response.

The way you ask a question reflects your mindset toward the person, situation, or task. Listen to your own questions. What do they tell you about your own mindset? Your questions also create a window into your team member's mindset. His or her answers will reveal his or her mindset, like history, assumptions, expectations, biases, and blind spots. These are valuable for you as a coach to see so you can more fully understand the employee's personal context within which he or she is operating. Equipped with this insight, you can adapt your questions and coaching approach.

Look at the subtle difference between these two questions:

1. Are you going to meet the new, shorter project deadline?
2. How might we meet the new, shorter project deadline?

Although these two questions are very similar, not only do they infer very different mindsets of the coach, but they also suggest very different options and degrees of openness to the employee. If you heard the first question, you would likely think you're in this alone, that there might not even be a possible solution, and if a solution exists, there is only one right answer. Alternatively, the second question uses a simple but powerful lead-in phrase, "How might we . . .". The word *how* infers that a solution exists, so we are now motivated to find it. The word *might* suggests there is more than one way to solve the problem, so we can be creative in our approach, and *we* infers that the team will find a solution. Clearly, the second approach to asking this question inspires greater motivation, engagement, and creativity.

Asking the right questions is at the core of a coach's role. So, be purposeful about the questions you ask, and be intentional about how you ask them to ignite engagement for your team.

POSITIVE COACHING HABIT SUMMARY

1 EXPLAIN Expectations

2 ASK Questions
- Define your objective *before* you ask.
- After you ask, be silent.
- Ask about timelines to meet deadlines.
- Manage how you ask, not just what you ask.

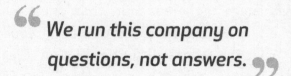

We run this company on questions, not answers.

—**ERIC SCHMIDT**
CEO, Google

TAKING ACTION

ASK Questions to Ignite Engagement

1. How can I ensure that I am asking purposeful questions? (E.g., before a meeting or team interaction, take a minute to define your objective, then use the table from this chapter to identify appropriate questions to ask.)

   _____

   _____

   _____

   _____

   _____

   _____

   _____

2. After I ask a question, what can I do to ensure that I am not filling silence before my team member can respond? (E.g., count to 10.)

   _____

   _____

   _____

   _____

   _____

   _____

   _____

CHAPTER 7

Positive Coaching Habit #3:

INVOLVE
Team to Enlist
Ownership

*Tell me and I'll forget; show me and I may
remember; involve me and I'll understand.*

—XUN KUANG
CONFUCIAN PHILOSOPHER

For years, leaders at the top of many organizations often had more knowledge than those on the front lines. Today, the game has changed. Technology has put knowledge in the hands of anyone with access to a computer or handheld device. Today, it's impossible for leaders to know it all. Plus, it is not in their own or in the organization's best interest to try. That's why you need to involve team members in finding solutions and innovations that improve products and services for your customers.

By asking your employees questions, you engage in a two-way information exchange. Ask team members to bring you solutions along with problems. People support what they help create. By involving employees, you enlist their ownership of issues and solutions. Some leaders feel threatened by the idea of involving their employees in identifying and solving problems. They believe they're giving up control over *how* their team will achieve its goals. However, inspiring coaches realize there is more than one way to solve a problem. An employee's approach might be different from the leader's, but the personal ownership that comes from being involved in the solution far outweighs any loss of control that a leader might feel. When employees are involved, the buck doesn't stop with you. It stops with each employee on the team. To continue to inspire winning results, involve your team in improving its work process and output.

Dashboard and Under-the-Hood Knowledge

A common misperception among leaders is that once you get to a certain level, you should consider only a 30,000-foot perspective (i.e., the big picture) of your business.

Although a high-level perspective is necessary for leadership success, it must be accompanied by an in-depth understanding of your team's operation (e.g., your drivers of cost, profit, quality, and customer satisfaction). When you make a habit of ignoring the little things, you eventually end up ignoring the big things. Don't misinterpret this as micromanagement. We are discussing leadership knowledge, not leadership activity.

Your car provides a helpful analogy for understanding the importance of both the big picture and detailed information. Just as your car's dashboard tells you speed, fuel level, and engine temperature, your organizational dashboard tells you if sales are up 5 percent, productivity is down, or project deliverables are on schedule. Leaders typically use dashboard knowledge.

While dashboard knowledge is important for understanding broad metrics and the general direction of your operation, it is less helpful for identifying specific actions, improvements, and adjustments that will help your team run more smoothly. For that kind of information, you have to look "under the hood." Looking under your car's hood provides insight into why your car is running hot, why it veers to the right, and why it's not starting as quickly as it should.

Under-the-hood knowledge about your team gives you specific information with respect to a given job, time, place, and set of circumstances. Inspiring coaches involve team members who possess under-the-hood knowledge. They understand that by the time a warning light on your dashboard starts blinking, you already have a problem under the hood. Your frontline team members then become your experts.

One of our clients, Bob Bunker, President and CEO of Lakeview Health, likes to harken back to his military days when he's looking under the hood. He refers to his field offices as the FEBA (Forward Edge of Battle Area). It's a vivid reminder to his corporate team that the field offices are where the business battle is won on a daily basis. Bunker has been known to spend much of his time on the FEBA listening to his field team and customers, and supporting both of them. He says, "Getting on the FEBA allows me to see and feel the daily processes and ponder process reengineering opportunities and technology applications, and better appreciate the interdependencies of our corporate and customer systems as a whole."[1] Involving his frontline team gives Bunker a more complete view of his business and enlists team ownership of the solutions. Inspiring coaches put their egos and assumptions aside to seek real-time input from team members who are working under the hood every day.

Think Small

Yuzo Yasuda's book featuring Toyota's idea system, *40 Years, 20 Million Ideas: The Toyota Suggestion System*, describes how Toyota had received one million ideas per year from its employees and had been doing so for more than a decade. More recently, Toyota received more than three million ideas from employees in one year.[2] Several other companies have also excelled at harnessing employee ideas and implementing them as a competitive advantage. Companies like Dana Corporation, Milliken & Company, Yamaha, Toshiba, Technicolor USA, Inc., and Boardroom, Inc. have each generated tens of thousands of ideas per year. Your first reaction to these staggering numbers of suggestions might be disbelief. This level of involvement is *not* achieved by using a suggestion box. It *is* achieved by engaging the minds of employees and tapping into their unlimited pool of ideas and creativity. Letting this resource go untapped is like sitting on top of a gold mine and feeling poor. So, how do these companies do it?

Before we answer that question, let's address *why* we should even focus on getting ideas when we are coaching. This coaching habit is not about ideas for ideas' sake. It is about soliciting ideas to improve employee productivity, reduce costs, increase speed, and eliminate waste. The primary objective is to improve individual and team performance. If done with a positive mindset and habits, we will also enhance relationships along the way. The by-product of this habit is a strong and rapid increase in the employees' sense of ownership. These under-the-hood ideas will ultimately make their work more interesting and efficient. Your team will realize cost savings, quality improvements, and service improvements that form an irreplaceable competitive advantage.

Okay, back to the question: How do they do it? The name of the game is to think small. Small ideas are actually better than big ideas because:

- Small ideas are much more likely to stay proprietary and create sustainable competitive advantage, since they are under-the-hood and situation-specific. Besides, your competitors are most likely looking for the next big idea. Let them wait for their grand slam while you hit a thousand singles.
- Small ideas enable you to focus on the details of your business. Excellence is the result of getting the details right. In many cases, it is literally impossible to improve performance (speed, service, quality, costs) beyond a certain level without small ideas.
- Small ideas help create a culture that values ideas (every idea is a good idea) and the people they come from, resulting in a boost in ownership at the grassroots level of your organization.

- Small ideas facilitate rapid and continuous organizational learning and performance improvements based on that learning.
- Small ideas are the best sources of big ideas. (The Post-it® note came from a small idea to find a better glue.)

Small ideas might include:

- "If we print our weekly status reports double-sided, we could save three reams of paper per month."
- "While I'm waiting for our driver to check in his shipment at our store's receiving dock, I sweep out the inside of his truck so he can make a quicker turn-around at our distribution center."
- "If I highlight off-plan line items on my report, the executive committee can more quickly and efficiently focus on those areas of concern."

Inspiring coaches go for quantity, not quality, of ideas to build a culture of innovation and ownership. They make ideas—lots of them—part of everyone's job. They use clarifying questions to determine if and how to best implement the ideas. Ask your team for the kinds of ideas you need. You may have a focus area for that week, month, or quarter. A good place to start is with the eight areas of waste. They spell TIM WOODS:

T **Transport**—Moving people, products, and information

I **Inventory**—Storing parts, pieces, and documentation ahead of requirements

M **Motion**—Bending, turning, reaching, lifting

W **Waiting**—For parts, information, instructions, equipment

O **Overproduction**—Making more than is immediately required

O **Over-processing**—Tighter tolerances or higher-grade materials than are needed

D **Defects**—Rework, scrap, incorrect/incomplete information

S **Skills**—Underutilizing capabilities, delegating tasks with inadequate training

Involve your team in addressing these areas of waste and other opportunities for improvement to enlist their ownership in the solution. One of our long-standing clients, Jeff Jensen, manages a portfolio of successful companies. Jeff has shared a favorite quote from his late father, Ron Jensen, who was an innovative and inspiring leader. He liked to say, "The biggest room in the world is the room for improvement." This metaphorical room for improvement can be your business, your team's processes, your team's skills, and most importantly, your own leadership.

Move Down to Coach Up

The biggest area for improvement is typically with "S", the Skills on your team. Underutilized skills are a hidden yet significant area of waste, and therefore, a big opportunity for you as the leader and coach. Start by appreciating that all employees are different and have different levels of potential. Just like your kids, you cannot view them as the same person with the same needs and potential. Inspiring coaches don't try to make everyone achieve at the same level; rather, they see it as their mission to help each employee reach his or her potential. To do so, when you address specific performance problems with employees, involve them in identifying the root cause of the problem and solutions to enlist their ownership in reaching their potential. Refer to the previous chapter, "Positive Coaching Habit #2: ASK Questions to Ignite Engagement," for questions to help you engage and involve employees in a coaching discussion to improve their skills.

When our son was 11 years old, he earned his junior black belt in karate. Of course, we were very proud of him, for he had come a very long way since his first lesson. We remember that first lesson well. He was 7 years old, and one of the first things the master instructor taught him was a simple exercise called a *kata*. This kata ended with him, the beginning student, saying emphatically, "V for victory and bow for humility," as he crisscrossed his arms over his head with fists clinched for the "V" and then bowed for humility.

That night, he came home from his lesson and quickly ran to us to proudly show us what he had learned. Seeing his enthusiasm, we dropped what we were doing and became an intent audience of two. As he finished the kata, he performed the closing: "V for victory and bow for humility!" he shouted. But then, to our surprise, he started yelling insults at us . . . "Man, I took you down! How about that, buddy?" and so on. More than a bit shocked and confused, we asked, "Hey pal, what was *that* all about?" He responded in a very matter-of-fact manner, "That's the bow for humility."

Well, his actions pointed out how such a little difference could make a BIG difference. He thought it was a bow for *humiliation*, not *humility*! Fear not. We clarified that definition before he earned his black belt. If we depend on others' perceptions to meet our expectations, we will be disappointed. Our son heard his instructor's performance expectation but made his own (incredibly misdirected) interpretation based on his own perceptions. The truth is we remember only 20 percent of what we hear.

Why is this percentage so low? Let's say you are hurried and swing by an employee's cube and say, "Grace, please make sure you use the new format on the month-end sales report . . . thanks." Even if Grace is a sharp employee, what do you think the chances are she will hear your request accurately, remember it, recall it accurately when it's relevant, interpret your instructions as you intended, and then perform the task satisfactorily? When we look at it this way, 20 percent sounds good.

Involving a team member in your coaching (versus just telling him or her what to do) minimizes re-coaching on the back end. If you are coaching employees on the same thing repeatedly, before you get frustrated with them, ask yourself:

- "Am I inspiring learning or am I just checking this off my list?"
- "Am I handing off a memo with instructions or am I asking the employee to perform a task while I give him or her real-time feedback?"

To help put into context the need to prevent re-coaching, the learning pyramid that follows illustrates that we generally remember:

10%
of what
we read
(books, e-mails,
blogs)

20%
of what we hear
(instructions)

30% of what we see
(looking at pictures)

50% of what we hear and see
(watching a movie, looking at an exhibit,
watching a demonstration)

70% of what we say
(participating in a discussion, giving a talk)

90% of what we both say and do
(simulating the real thing, doing the real thing)

In the example with our son, he heard his performance expectation (20 percent chance of remembering) but made his own interpretations from there. Well, this happens on your team every day, and it's up to you to ensure effective coaching of your team. Create a habit of pushing down the learning pyramid to coach up your team and you are on your way to victory.

Zig Ziglar had a famous quote: *"You can have everything in life you want, if you will help enough other people get what they want."* This holds true for your team. It's not about who gets the credit. It's not about who is the leader. It's about helping your team members accomplish their goals. In that way, everyone wins.

POSITIVE COACHING HABIT SUMMARY

❶ EXPLAIN Expectations

❷ ASK Questions

❸ INVOLVE Team
- Seek under-the-hood knowledge from your team.
- Think small—quantity over quality of ideas.
- Solicit ideas to improve the eight areas of waste.
- Move down the learning pyramid to coach up your team.

> ❝ *Great things in business are never done by one person. They're done by a team of people.* ❞
>
> **—STEVE JOBS**
> Cofounder, Apple, Inc.

TAKING ACTION

INVOLVE Team to Enlist Ownership

1. How can I regularly seek my team's input and involve them in making improvements?

_____

_____

_____

_____

_____

_____

_____

_____

2. How can I adjust my coaching approach to push down the learning pyramid and prevent re-coaching?

_____

_____

_____

_____

_____

_____

_____

_____

CHAPTER 8

Positive Coaching Habit #4:

MEASURE
Results to Boost
Accountability

What gets measured gets done.

—PETER DRUCKER
PIONEER OF MODERN BUSINESS PRACTICES

Have you ever noticed the intensity difference when you play a game for fun compared to "playing for keeps"? Our family and friends frequently play Ping-Pong in our game room. It's a fun and easy game for all ages. We can see the Ping-Pong table from our kitchen. When the players are just warming up, you notice their relaxed stance, the slow rhythmic sound of the ball hitting each paddle, and then the brief silence after a shot is missed. As soon as they start keeping score, there are visible changes. Each player is now slightly crouched down with eyes wide open looking straight ahead, the rhythm of the ball is faster and louder, and a missed shot is usually accompanied with a cheer or a groan of agony. Scorekeeping generates greater intensity, better focus, more energy, and more winning shots. You can observe the same in any sport. And you can certainly observe the same dynamic on your team.

Keeping score brings out our best because we inherently like to win. You must keep score to know whether you're winning, or you can easily end up with your team being very active but not very productive. You can keep score on your revenue, profitability, customer satisfaction, quality, prospect pipeline, cost per sales, employee engagement, defects, inventory, call-center response time, and so on. There certainly is no lack of things to measure. To keep it simple, measure only what matters most. Do not measure everything. You can use the 80/20 principle here. Which 20 percent of the measures tell you 80 percent of the story? Those are the measures you want to track. Of course, if you're going to keep score, you need a scoreboard. You will want to design a scoreboard that is simple and clear, resonates with your team, and is easy to update.

All work is a process and all processes can be measured in one or more ways. Performance measures fall into five categories:

1. **Quantity.** Number of units produced, tasks completed, calls made, proposals submitted, invoices processed, etc.
2. **Quality.** Completeness and accuracy in agreed-to product or service specifications.
3. **Timeliness.** Hitting agreed-to deadlines or milestones.
4. **Cost.** Dollar amount budgeted for a given product, service, project, process, initiative, and event.
5. **Manner of performance.** Behavior, approach, and/ or attitude demonstrated while performing the task. This metric will be addressed later in this chapter.

Lagging and Leading Indicators

Inspiring coaches also balance their view by looking at both lagging and leading indicators of performance. Every team has a variety of performance indicators. Teams that adhere to their plans understand the different types of indicators, what they mean and, most importantly, how to balance them.

Consider a measurement continuum. The two ends represent the two types of performance indicators. Lagging indicators are the results of your team's *past* performance—they enable you to see if your activities produced the desired outcomes. Leading indicators are the drivers of your team's *future* performance—they give you early warning signs of problems.

Financial Measures	Customer* Measures	Process Measures	Employee Measures
• Revenues • Costs • Profits	• Complaint resolution • Customer satisfaction • Customer retention *Internal & external	• Quality • Cycle time • Productivity • Response time	• Employee satisfaction • Employee development • Employee retention

Lagging Indicators   *Leading Indicators*

⟵──────────────────────────────────────⟶

Past   Future

John Walker is chief financial officer for VIRA Insight, a global manufacturer of retail fixtures. Walker is particularly skilled at balancing the measures he tracks. In talking with him, Walker summed it up like this: "If you want to know what's going on in your business, talk to your customer service reps and your collections reps."[1] Walker understands these two functions offer direct customer information from opposite ends (lagging and leading) of the customer life cycle.

Economic and competitive pressures force many leaders to focus on lagging indicators, typically financial ones. Of course, it's important to consider lagging indicators to know how well you have performed in the past. However, you must balance your view with leading indicators that indicate how your organization will perform 6, 9, or 12 months from now. A singular focus on lagging indicators gives you little opportunity for corrective action if your team drifts off course. Look at both lagging and leading indicators of performance. This balanced view enables you to know what *did* happen and also anticipate what *will* happen.

For example, a company that sells software to manage computer assets was growing so fast the company became enamored with their revenue growth (a lagging indicator) to the exclusion of leading indicators, such as employee development and service quality. Since their investors were happy, this focus solely on lagging indicators went on for nearly two years. As a result, the company thought the light they saw at the end of the tunnel was their bright future. Instead, it was an oncoming train. The company's meteoric rise was matched only by its swift decline. Because employees were not being trained and developed, they were either ill-equipped to take on new responsibilities or disillusioned. Some employees left the company, and those who remained were not able to maintain expected quality levels. This took little time to translate into lower customer satisfaction which, in a very competitive market, quickly resulted in much lower customer retention. And we all know what happens to revenues when we lose customers. Unfortunately, in this case, even a diligent rebalancing of the company's view and the resulting corrective action was too little, too late.

As the captain of your team's ship, keep a balanced view of your team's performance to increase your competency and adhere to your plan. Chart your course (high-level perspective) and ensure the deck is clean (details). While on your journey, check the wake of your ship (lagging indicators) and keep an eye on the horizon ahead (leading indicators).

Compelling Scoreboards

Your scoreboard doesn't have to be a lackluster summary of your monthly business report showing key measures. It's a chance to be creative and visual with your team. Use your scoreboard to tell a clear and compelling story in as few words and numbers as possible. Consider some of these scoreboard formats:

- Visual thermometer with a rising mercury line to show progress.
- Traffic light (red, yellow, and green indicators to show if you are off-plan, slightly off-plan, or on-plan, respectively).
- A jar of jellybeans to illustrate percentage of completion.

- Emoticons ☺☻ or visual indicators, such as thumbs up/thumbs down, next to each goal. These emoticons work great for movie reviews and Facebook, so why not use them to help your team quickly see the score?
- A picture of an actual scoreboard to keep track of number of calls made, new customers, shipments, invoices processed, response time, customer complaints, new hires, or whichever metrics are most important to your team.

Keeping your scoreboard updated is critical. Your scoreboard must be current to be compelling and be seen as a valid reflection of performance. Understanding what is happening on your team empowers you to adjust continually, enhance accountability, and boost results.

Inspiring coaches get creative with scoreboards while keeping them relevant to the employees they are managing. For example, Stephen Mansfield, CEO of Methodist Health System in Dallas, has a handy technique to keep his team focused and accountable. His scorecard is literally just that—an index card. Mansfield says, "I have a little handwritten index card for each direct report. On that card, I write the three primary things that person and I have agreed that I most need from them. I check in with each person every few weeks to ask how he or she is doing on those items. I always end the discussion with, 'Is there anything I can do to help?'"[2] Mansfield is a master at boosting accountability for results and developing great relationships by measuring progress and results. Notice in his quote that he is also asking his team what *he* can do. This is a good example of how to integrate the five coaching habits into the team's daily interactions.

Spotify uses a technology solution to gamify its measurement of performance. They wanted to make the mundane chore of employee performance reviews not only exciting and engaging, but productive—as in, raising performance levels. They used a Salesforce.com product called Rypple, which uses gamification to create a social network platform that enables employee feedback in real time. When a Spotify team member hits a goal, the entire company can see it along with the virtual "badge" and high-five from the manager. This recognition then produces in-house conversation feeds from colleagues and other managers.

"Everyone at Spotify—every individual, every team, every department—has a quarterly target," said Johan Persson, Spotify's organizational development manager. "These [targets] are published and shared within the company, so everyone can find, browse, explore, understand what's going on, feel connected to what's happening and reach out if they find something interesting."[3] When targets are hit or missed, everyone knows. Rather than waiting until the end of the year, employees know where they stand every day.

Measure Results and Behavior

When someone performs well or poorly, your job is to *involve the employee* (Habit #3) in finding out why so he or she can either double down on the cause of good performance or address the cause of poor performance. Most leaders tend to focus their critique, feedback, and training on symptoms rather than the root cause of poor performance. This ends up wasting time and resources. If you directly address the root cause, you will see immediate results. The fastest way to identify the cause is to closely observe performance, the work system and *ask questions* (Habit #2).

To get a more complete picture of performance, measure your team members' results and behavior. Achieving the performance standard on one of them is necessary but not sufficient to be a winning performer. Getting results is great, but they will not be sustainable without the right behaviors. Wrong behaviors include being a poor teammate by not sharing information and resources, acting inconsistently with team and organizational values, or disregarding agreed-to job processes (e.g., conducting quality checks, making "X" number of calls, using prescribed materials). Any of these behaviors puts your team's results and culture at risk. On the other hand, acceptable behaviors do not necessarily guarantee results, so measuring both is key to continually improving performance.

You get the behaviors you're willing to tolerate. If you rank your team by performance level, your lowest performer is a public statement of the performance level that you're willing to tolerate. That is what your team sees as your performance standard. Ignoring issues puts your team and your leadership credibility at risk. A small molehill-sized issue today that takes five minutes to proactively address can quickly expand into a mountain-sized matter that requires five days or more to resolve. Remember that phrase about unexpressed emotions from Chapter 4, "Know Your Emotions"? The same applies here. Unaddressed performance matters do not just go away; instead, they eventually rear their heads in uglier ways.

In the following 2 × 2 matrix, you can see how the four combinations of measuring results and behaviors affect your coaching approach:

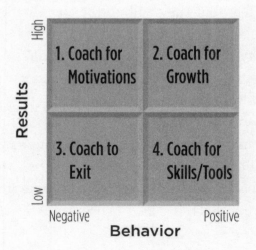

Quadrant 1 is the employee whose results are up to standard, but whose behavior is not. These are the trickiest coaching situations because the employee is delivering results but his or her behavior is creating risk for the team. Focus on the behavioral motivations of the employee and be clear that you have an "and/both" not an "either/or" expectation; results and behaviors must meet the standard. This is where some leaders put their integrity at risk—by tolerating the bull in the china shop because he or she delivers results, even though it might put the team at risk.

Quadrant 2 employees are your stars, delivering results and doing it the right way. Encourage and look for opportunities to expand this employee's responsibilities and influence.

Quadrant 3 employees are not well suited for the role. Therefore, after appropriate coaching and support with no improvement on either performance dimension, don't waste any time moving them out. You should make your personnel decisions with rationality, but implement them with humanity.

Coach Quadrant 4 employees on the skills and tools needed to deliver results. They are likely willing to learn since they are already meeting your behavior standards. That said, be clear and specific with your language and improvement expectations. Keep it simple with the 3 *W* format that we discussed in Chapter 5, "Positive Coaching

Habit #1: EXPLAIN Expectations to Gain Alignment." Let these employees know what needs to improve, who is responsible, and by when.

Stephen Covey said, *"The main thing is to keep the main thing the main thing."*[4] When employees understand what the main thing is and have a clear concept of what is required of them, measurements can become their friends. Measurements are encouraging and validating to high-performing employees and provide an objective case to improve for lower-performing employees.

POSITIVE COACHING HABIT SUMMARY

1 **EXPLAIN Expectations**

2 **ASK Questions**

3 **INVOLVE Team**

4 **MEASURE Results**
- Measure what matters most.
- Balance lagging and leading indicators.
- Create compelling scoreboards.
- Measure results and behavior.

Feedback is the breakfast of champions.

—KEN BLANCHARD
Author, *The One Minute-Manager*

TAKING ACTION

MEASURE Results to Boost Accountability

1. What are two key measures of success for each of my team members?

_____

_____

_____

_____

_____

_____

_____

2. What is the simplest, real-time method to keep score for my team?

_____

_____

_____

_____

_____

_____

_____

_____

CHAPTER 9

Positive Coaching Habit #5:

APPRECIATE
People to Deepen
Commitment

Everyone has an invisible sign hanging from their neck saying, "Make me feel important." Never forget this message when working with people.

—MARY KAY ASH
FOUNDER, MARY KAY COSMETICS

William James, the father of American psychology, stated that the most fundamental psychological need is to be appreciated. We want to feel fully appreciated for our work. Unfortunately, the reality is that lack of appreciation is the No. 1 reason people leave their jobs. The direct supervisor is the primary source of appreciation (or lack thereof), the primary influencer of job satisfaction and engagement, and a primary reason people either leave or stay on the job.

Showing appreciation is a common blind spot for leaders—and for people in any relationship, for that matter. You no doubt feel appreciative of your team; yet predictably there is a gap between how much your team feels appreciated and how much you feel that you appreciate them. Why is that? This disconnect exists because you likely don't convert every thought of appreciation into visible acts of appreciation. While we judge ourselves by our intentions, others judge us by our actions. What is important is not how much you appreciate people, but rather how much you *demonstrate* your appreciation.

A survey of 15 million people worldwide illuminates the business benefits of appreciation. This Gallup study by Tom Rath and Donald O. Clifton found that people who receive regular recognition at work:

- Experience increased productivity;
- Enjoy increased engagement with colleagues;
- Are more likely to stay with the organization;
- Receive higher loyalty and satisfaction scores from customers;
- Have better safety records and fewer accidents on the job.[1]

Appreciation comes down to basic psychology:

- Reinforce those behaviors that you want to see more frequently.
- Look for opportunities to recognize and appreciate your team's efforts and results.
- Catch the team doing something right . . . and encourage them to do it often.

Demonstrating appreciation is not a matter of time and intention. It's a matter of priority and action.

Know the Person Behind the Employee

Never assume you know what motivates someone. Appreciation is certainly not a one-size-fits-all coaching habit. It should be customized to each employee, so personalize it. For example, being recognized at an all-employee meeting might trigger more perspiration than inspiration for an introverted employee. Instead, use the information you learn about your employees to present an appropriate gift, token, or sincere expression of appreciation. Your gesture will be less important than the obvious time and thoughtfulness that went into it.

When our oldest daughter was in kindergarten, we recall her coming home from school in tears because she was told to sit in the teacher's chair. She was normally very well behaved, so we spoke to her teacher to understand what had happened. The teacher looked at us with confusion on her face. Then she explained that our daughter was rewarded for her good behavior with a chance to sit in the teacher's chair. What the giver perceives as appreciation and recognition might not be aligned with how the recipient receives it. So, you must know your people and what motivates them before you can personalize your appreciation.

Learn something new each day about one of your employees. Keep a file at your desk, on your computer, or on your cell phone with a few key notes about each team member's hobbies, favorite things, and family. Then weave this information into your interactions with your employees and recognition for them. If you know a team member has bad allergies, you can avoid giving her tickets to the local botanical gardens as a thank you. If you know that same person is a foodie, you can intentionally select a nice restaurant the next time you have a business lunch. Your team will return your personalized appreciation with deeper personal commitment and discretionary effort. Know your people, not just your employees. You will begin to understand them more fully and be able to more effectively express your appreciation.

To ignite commitment, appreciate not only good performance, but also appreciate the person. It is easy to appreciate the top performers who bail you out of tight spots or whose hard work makes you look good. It is more challenging, but very meaningful, to appreciate the person. You can appreciate: service to others outside of work, consistently professional demeanor or attire, integrity in gray situations, willingness to coach new team members, optimistic outlook, or ability to keep personal challenges at home and remain focused on the job.

Appreciate Progress

A positive coach appreciates results *and* progress. We often hear leaders say that they will appreciate their teams once a certain goal is achieved. These leaders do not understand the power of appreciating successive approximations.

Let's illustrate this powerful concept this way. Imagine you're trying to teach your new puppy to roll over. If you wait for the puppy to just coincidentally roll over to reward him, you might be waiting a very long time, and it likely will never happen. However, if you reward your puppy each time he just lays on his side, an act that approximates the desired behavior, you're one step closer to your goal. Next, he might roll to his back and you reinforce him again. These are successive approximations of the desired behavior. Before you know it, your puppy is rolling over.

This dynamic is mirrored in human behavior. If you look for and appreciate small acts that start to approximate the end goal, you will accelerate progress toward the goal. For example, a team member has a sales goal of closing 10 deals by the end of the quarter. If you wait until the end of the quarter, you will have missed the opportunity to positively shape behavior and results. If you notice this team member made the targeted 50 calls today, you can appreciate that initial step and increase the chances he or she will make the targeted number of calls the next day. People do more for those who appreciate them and they do more of the behavior they are appreciated for. This is a powerful human dynamic that inspiring coaches know how to leverage. By the same token, if your team member makes only 25 calls in a day, you have an opportunity to encourage him or her and discuss how the call volume, if not improved, will directly influence the results. This addresses the Circle of Consequences we described in Chapter 5, "Positive Coaching Habit #1: EXPLAIN Expectations to Gain Alignment."

Resist the temptation of thinking that your team will get soft if you appreciate them too much. Don't wait for the end goal. Frequently appreciate progress toward goals. As long as your appreciation is sincere and specific, we have never found any research whatsoever that show employees have felt overappreciated.

Sincere and Specific

After interviewing 25,000 leaders, Ferdinand Fournies found the most effective leaders had one thing in common—they expressed a sincere interest in their employees.[2] "Sincere" is the operative word here. Your motivation matters! If you appreciate employees in hopes of getting something in return, they will see right through you.

You have complete control over your appreciation. No budget limitations or excuses here. There are literally thousands of ways to demonstrate your appreciation at little or no cost. You can occasionally offer a gift card or something of modest value, but you should rely more on your creativity and knowledge of the employee to personalize your appreciation so that it is meaningful. The key to appreciation is making it sincere and specific. Don't fall into the trap of blurting out the robotic "Good job." Take the time to explain *why* you appreciate an employee's performance, such as, "I really appreciate the way you kept our customer happy without incurring more cost." Then, tell the employee how his or her performance made you feel. Are your satisfied, excited, proud, impressed? Finally, encourage the employee to keep doing the same specific behavior. If adjustments need to be made, address that in a separate conversation.

Do you remember a time you received a card or note of thanks from your boss? Did you throw it out? Probably not. In our work at client organizations, we have seen more than a few handwritten notes of appreciation on employees' desks. Often these cards are several years old (five years in one case), yet still prominently and proudly displayed. We often wonder if the leaders who wrote them understand how much discretionary effort their three-minute investment yielded or know how meaningful those cards were to those employees.

Not everyone is a notecard writer, but every leader has a way of showing appreciation that feels authentic. Daniel Jones is Chairman, President, and CEO of Encore Wire, a publicly traded leader in the copper wire industry for over 25 years. He says, "Even as the world has become more high-tech, I have continued to send employees handwritten notes of appreciation. Based on the feedback, I am convinced that the personal touch has even greater impact with today's worker."[3] Jones's testimony reinforces that we work in a high-tech world, but leadership is still a "high-touch" job.

The number of ways to express your appreciation is only limited by your imagination. Inspiring coaches find ways to outthink the competition, not outspend them. Here are just a few ways you can appreciate a team member:

- **Say "Thank You!"** This is an all-too-obvious yet highly underused form of appreciation.
- **Allow employees to present their work to your boss.** This is a great way to engage employees, and it also shows *your* boss what kind of leader you are.
- **Offer team members a choice of projects to work on.** When employees buy into a project, they will put their hearts into it.
- **Put a sincere acknowledgment in your company or department newsletter.** This takes only a few minutes of your time but creates long-term "trophy value" for the employee.
- **Tell an employee's story of accomplishment at a staff meeting.** Stories are perceived as more interesting, meaningful, thoughtful, and memorable.
- **Take a team member to lunch to show your appreciation.** Remember to do more listening than talking.

Employee appreciation goes a long way. In the midst of many other problems at work, employees will remain loyal and committed if they feel like they are valued and recognized. Your ROIT (return on invested time) is higher than nearly any other investment you can make, resulting in a team that is committed to your goals and committed to you as a leader.

Three Words to Deepen Commitment

Some people literally change the world for good—people like Gandhi, Mother Teresa, Abraham Lincoln, and Thomas Edison. Although it's an ambitious goal to change the world, we often underestimate our singular power to positively change the world of those around us. Each of us has the power to change someone's world with the gift of encouragement. We don't even have to *do* anything! We only have to *say* three simple words. Try one of these three-word, power-packed statements to change a team member's world:

- *I appreciate you.*
- *You are talented.*
- *I trust you.*
- *I promise you.* (Then keep it!)
- *Take a chance.*
- *You will succeed.*
- *I am sorry.*
- *I can help.*
- *I understand you.*
- *I believe you.*
- *You will succeed.*
- *You inspire me.*

Whether it's a long conversation with an employee, colleague, boss, friend, or relative, or simply placing an order at a restaurant, every word makes a difference. The results of our interactions are rarely neutral; they are almost always positive or negative. Ask yourself: "Do my words reflect my passion to encourage others, create win-wins, continuously learn, embrace change, and support my team's success?"

Positive, encouraging words are the seeds of commitment. Once they are spoken, they grow into results. Whether those results become apparent sooner or later when we speak words of encouragement we can expect victory. Plant the seeds of success in someone's mind and heart today. You'll start a positive ripple effect that will be felt by many people and many miles away, not to mention the positive effect you will feel inside.

Leverage "The Yellow Car Phenomenon" we described in the Chapter 1, "Know Your Thoughts," to help you appreciate your team. Simply make good performance your Yellow Car. Look for things they are doing well, look for positive progress, and look for positive traits. For example:

- Presenting a professional image;
- Looking for win-win solutions;
- Encouraging team members;
- Staying focused at work when they have lots of distractions at home;
- Consistently meeting deadlines or presenting top-quality work.

Give what you want, and you will get what you need. Get to know the person behind the employee, appreciate progress, appreciate sincerely and specifically, and use encouraging words. These simple actions will ignite positive commitment on your team.

POSITIVE COACHING HABIT SUMMARY

❶ EXPLAIN Expectations

❷ ASK Questions

❸ INVOLVE Team

❹ MEASURE Results

❺ APPRECIATE People
- Know the person behind the employee.
- Appreciate progress.
- Be sincere and specific.
- Use three words to encourage.

> *People will forget what you said. They will even forget what you did. But they will never forget how you made them feel.*
>
> **—MAYA ANGELOU**
> American poet

TAKING ACTION

APPRECIATE People to Deepen Commitment

1. What one thought of appreciation can I convert into an act of appreciation today?

_____

_____

_____

_____

_____

_____

_____

2. What personal reminder system can I use to ensure I regularly appreciate my team's progress?

_____

_____

_____

_____

_____

_____

_____

The 5 Positive Coaching Habits At-a-Glance

POSITIVE COACHING HABIT	RESULT	TOOLS
❶ EXPLAIN Expectations	Alignment	• Answer the Fundamental Four Questions (goals, plans, roles, and rewards). • Align on the 3 W's—*What, Who,* and *When.* • Explain the fourth *W, Why,* using the Circle of Consequences. • Learn along the way: Debrief after interactions, meetings, presentations, milestones.
❷ ASK Questions	Engagement	• Define your objective before you ask. • After you ask, be silent. • Ask about timelines to meet deadlines. • Manage how you ask, not just what you ask.
❸ INVOLVE Team	Ownership	• Seek under-the-hood knowledge from your team. • Think small—quantity over quality of ideas. • Solicit ideas to improve the eight areas of waste. • Move down the learning pyramid to coach up your team.
❹ MEASURE Results	Accountability	• Measure what matters most. • Balance lagging and leading indicators. • Create compelling scoreboards. • Measure results and behavior.
❺ APPRECIATE People	Commitment	• Know the person behind the employee. • Appreciate progress. • Be sincere and specific. • Use three words to encourage.

Take a free, three-minute self-assessment of positive coaching mindset and habits at: www.theLgroup.com/PositiveCoaching

PART III

Your Coaching Game Plan

66 *I have been impressed with the urgency of doing. Knowing is not enough; we must apply. Being willing is not enough; we must do.* 99

—LEONARDO DA VINCI

The poem titled *"Who am I?,"* by an unknown author, serves as a poignant introduction to this chapter:

I am your constant companion.
I am your greatest helper or heaviest burden.
I will push you onward or drag you down to failure.
I am completely at your command.
Half of the things you do you might just as well turn over to me,
and I will be able to do them—quickly and correctly.

I am easily managed—you must be firm with me.
Show me exactly how you want something done,
and after a few lessons, I will do it automatically.

I am the servant of all great people,
and alas, of all failures as well.
Those who are great, I have made great.
Those who are failures, I have made failures.

I am not a machine though
I work with the precision of a machine
plus the intelligence of a person.
You may run me for a profit or turn me for ruin—
it makes no difference to me.

Take me, train me, be firm with me, and
I will place the world at your feet.
Be easy with me and I will destroy you.
WHO AM I?
I AM HABIT.

Nearly half of your daily activities are habitual, for better or for worse. You don't think about them, you just do them. You have simple, decades-old habits, like brushing your teeth, that you don't have to think about. You also have more modern habits like waking up and instinctively grabbing your cell phone to check your e-mail and texts.

As we mentioned earlier, we have great respect for Olympic athletes. They start with the right mindset and they develop the habits necessary to achieve their goals. They also have a game plan when they step onto the court, ice, field, or track—specific strategies to put their mindset and habits into action. The same holds true when it comes to coaching and inspiring your team. How do you put a positive coaching mindset and the five positive coaching habits into action to yield winning results and relationships? You need a coaching game plan.

Plan to Win

The key to finishing big is to start small. Big achievements like running a marathon, introducing a new product, or exceeding a hefty sales goal all start with one small step. Consistent "baby steps" lead to BIG places. The same holds true when you are embracing new habits to inspire your team. As we discussed in Part I, "Positive Coaching Mindset," an important first step is to know yourself. Your strengths can't benefit you if you don't know how to leverage them. By the same token, your greatest liability is the one you're unaware of. So, stop right now and complete a three-minute positive coaching self-assessment at www.theLgroup.com/PositiveCoaching.

Your real-time feedback report will help you immediately in two ways:

- First, the assessment will identify your baseline, your starting point, by measuring your coaching mindset and habits.
- Second, it will identify initial steps you can take to elevate your coaching.

The whirlwind of daily demands tends to push us toward poor habits, such as being reactive versus proactive. These daily pressures can make us feel like one of the rats in behaviorist B. F. Skinner's famous lab experiments. We are confronted with what feels like an urgent situation (stimulus) and we jump at it (response). The immediate focus on daily transactions also makes it more challenging to keep a positive coaching mindset and use the positive coaching habits, robbing us of opportunities to transform others through coaching.

The great thing about being human (aside from our ability to use a TV remote) is that we can exercise choice.

Unlike Skinner's rats, our human behavior equation is: Stimulus → *Choice* → Response.

The challenge is that sometimes we move so fast that we speed right past our choice. We simply react to the multitude of stimuli-demanding customers, boss's deadlines, screaming kids, requests to volunteer, web page pop-up ads, Facebook status changes, e-mail notifications, GPS voices telling you to "veer right," text tones, and on and on. So how do you take charge of your choices and habits?

Start by reflecting on specific triggers that may prevent you from sticking to the positive coaching habits. For example, when you feel stressed, do you tend to tell your team what to do instead of asking for their input? Are there times when your team is doing well and things are going smoothly, maybe too smoothly for you to feel comfortable, so you find something trivial the team could improve instead of appreciating its performance? Another trigger could be that when meetings run long, you start to feel rushed, so you do not wrap up with the 3 *W*'s (*What, Who,* and *When*) to ensure that the team is aligned on expectations.

Write down your triggers and look at them relative to the results from the Positive Coaching self-assessment. Is there a connection between your triggers and the areas where you scored lowest? Next, write a specific action you will take to neutralize or avoid your triggers so you can consistently apply the five coaching habits.

Inspiring leaders and coaches never lose sight of the "C"—choice. The choice is yours. Success can occasionally be accidental, but excellence is never accidental. Choose to lead, coach, and excel intentionally.

Good Student—Great Coach

Coaching is not just about investing in others; it's also about investing in yourself. When you grow, you can better help others grow. And when you help others grow, you grow. It's a positive upward spiral. The key to being a great coach is to be a good student. It all starts with you. Inspiring coaches are lifelong and everyday learners. They never feel like they have "arrived." Consider this insight from Henry Ford, Sr.:

None of our men are "experts." We have most unfortunately found it necessary to get rid of a man as soon as he thinks himself an expert because no one ever considers himself expert if he really knows his job. A man who knows a job sees so much more to be done than he has done, that he is always pressing forward and never gives up an instant of thought to how good and how efficient he is. Thinking always ahead, thinking always of trying to do more, brings a state of mind in which nothing is impossible. The moment one gets into the "expert" state of mind a great number of things become impossible.

Inspiring coaches have a growth mindset. They believe their talents can be developed through constant learning, hard work, good strategies, and input from others. Microsoft CEO Satya Nadella succeeded the notoriously combative Steve Ballmer. Nadella has dramatically revived Microsoft's reputation and its relevance by emphasizing collaboration. He has ignited what he calls a "learn-it-all" culture versus the company's historical "know-it-all" culture. As senior editor Harry McCracken explains in "Microsoft Rewrites the Code," the results have been eye-popping: more than $250 billion in market value gains in less than four years—a feat that, quantitatively, puts Nadella in the pantheon of Bezos–Cook–Page–Zuckerberg.[1]

Your team looks to you as its role model for leading and learning. What do they see? Does it look to them like you know it all, like you're stuck in the past or like you're just cruising? If your team sees your thirst for learning, they will model the same behavior. Your continual learning hones your competence . . . and competence builds confidence. Confidence is critical; inspiring coaches need it, and their teams want to see it.

Today more than ever, there is a "leadership lab" of learning activities and opportunities available to help you build your leadership skills and refine your coaching mindset. There is a treasure trove of knowledge about leadership and coaching at your fingertips, literally. But there is more to learn than just what you can read on the Internet.

You can find best coaching practices everywhere. Observe the coaches in your life. You can find nuggets of coaching excellence from a parent or in-law, a clergy person, a speaker at a professional association meeting, a fellow leader, your child's school principal, a scout troop leader, or a particularly helpful salesperson at a local department store. Watch, ask, listen, and learn.

There are also lessons to be learned in everything your team does. Look for learning opportunities in post-project reviews, customer meetings, conflicts with other departments, changes in priorities, miscommunications, and mistakes. Seize all these experiences to build your coaching mindset and skill set.

Another way to elevate your coaching game is to glean wisdom from mentors. Mentors offer you a precious glimpse into their life experiences. If experience truly is the best teacher, then you would be wise to study the life lessons and expertise of a mentor.

For the greatest benefit, seek out mentors with the specific skills you desire to acquire. Maybe it's the company's top strategist, the salesperson with the magnetic people skills, the teammate who consistently wows the

> *It's what you learn after you know it all that counts.*
>
> **—JOHN WOODEN**
> Former UCLA Basketball Coach and 10-Time National Champion

crowd with presentations, or the executive who everyone wants to work for. Target their strengths and learn what makes them the best in their area. As your goals evolve or you enter a new stage of your career, your mentors will naturally change. Be prepared to end mentoring relationships (always with appreciation) and be willing to initiate new ones.

The brilliant scientist Albert Einstein once said, "Intellectual growth should commence at birth and cease only at death." Wise words. Never stop learning. Take the time to invest in yourself so you can invest well in others.

Commit to Your Team, Not Yourself

We tend to view a commitment to others as deeper and stronger than a commitment to ourselves, in part because it creates more public accountability. Remember that coaching is about others, not you. Reflect on why maintaining the five coaching habits is important to your team members, personally and professionally.

Every time you apply one of the coaching habits, you're enhancing a team member's life, which creates a positive ripple effect throughout your business and customers.

Conversely, every time you choose to say "yes" to some other activity and forgo one of the coaching habits, you're robbing that same team member of the opportunity to grow, contribute, and succeed. Also, the beneficiaries of that growth, contribution and success are robbed of the positive impact they might have received.

You're the leadership pebble in the lake of many people's lives. So, find your own compelling purpose for making a positive coaching mindset and the positive coaching habits part of your daily leadership. Then be bold enough to share your commitment with your team.

Leave a Positive Legacy

Inheritance is what we leave *to* others. Legacy is what we leave *in* them. Here is one of our favorite, true stories of living and leaving a legacy.

In the early 1900s, Al Capone virtually owned Chicago. Capone wasn't famous for anything heroic. He was notorious for entangling "the Windy City" in everything from bootlegged booze and prostitution to murder.

Capone had a lawyer, nicknamed "Easy Eddie." He was Capone's lawyer for a good reason. Eddie was very good at what he did. In fact, Eddie's skill at legal maneuvering kept Big Al out of jail for a long time. To show his appreciation, Capone paid him very well.

Not only was the money big, but Eddie also got special dividends. For instance, he and his family occupied a fenced-in mansion with live-in help and all of the conveniences of the day. The estate was so large it filled an entire Chicago city block.

Eddie lived the high life of the Chicago mob, but he did have one soft spot. He had a son he loved dearly, and Eddie saw to it that his young son had the best of everything, including clothes, cars, and a good education. Nothing was withheld, and price was no object.

Despite his involvement with organized crime, Eddie tried to teach his son right from wrong. Eddie wanted him to be a better man than he was. Yet with all his wealth and influence, there were two things he couldn't give his son: He couldn't pass on a good name and he couldn't set a good example.

> *Alone we can do so little, together we can do so much.*
> —HELEN KELLER

One day, Easy Eddie reached a difficult decision. Wanting to rectify wrongs he had done, he decided he would go to the authorities and tell the truth about Al "Scarface" Capone, clean up his tarnished name, and offer his son some semblance of integrity. To do this, he would have to testify against the Mob, and he knew that the cost would be great. So, he testified. Within the year, Easy Eddie's life ended in a blaze of gunfire on a lonely Chicago street. He died knowing he had given his son the greatest gift he had to offer, at the greatest price he would ever pay.

Fast-forward to World War II, a war that produced many heroes. One such man was Lieutenant Commander Butch O'Hare. He was a fighter pilot assigned to the aircraft carrier *Lexington* in the South Pacific.

One day, his entire squadron was sent on a mission. After he was airborne, he looked at his fuel gauge and realized that someone had forgotten to top off his fuel tank. He would not have enough fuel to complete his mission and get back to his ship. His flight leader told him to return to the carrier. Reluctantly, he dropped out of formation and headed back to the fleet. As he was returning to the mother ship he saw something that turned his blood cold. A squadron of Japanese aircraft was speeding their way toward the American fleet.

With the American squadron gone on a sortie, the fleet was all but defenseless. Butch couldn't reach his squadron and bring them back in time to save the fleet. Nor could he warn the fleet of the approaching danger. There was only one thing to do. He must somehow divert them from the fleet.

Laying aside all thoughts of personal safety, he dove into the formation of Japanese planes. Wing-mounted 50 calibers blazed as he charged in, attacking one surprised enemy plane and then another. Butch wove in and out of the now broken Japanese formation and fired at as many planes as possible until all his ammunition was finally spent. Undaunted, he continued the assault.

He dove at the planes, trying to clip a wing or tail in hopes of damaging as many enemy planes as possible and rendering them unfit to fly. Finally, the exasperated Japanese squadron took off in another direction.

Deeply relieved, Butch O'Hare and his tattered fighter limped back to the carrier. Upon arrival he reported in and related the event surrounding his return. The film from the gun-camera mounted on his plane told the tale. It showed the extent of Butch's daring attempt to protect his fleet. He had, in fact, destroyed five enemy aircraft. This took place on February 20, 1942, and for that action Butch became the Navy's first Ace of World War II and the first Naval aviator to win the Congressional Medal of Honor. A year later Butch was killed in aerial combat at the age of 29.

His hometown would not allow the memory of this World War II hero to fade, and today, O'Hare Airport in Chicago is named in tribute to the courage of this great man. So, the next time you find yourself at O'Hare International, visit Butch's memorial displaying his statue and his Medal of Honor.

So, what do these two stories have to do with each other?

Butch O'Hare was Edward (Easy Eddie) J. O'Hare's son. Despite knowing the dire consequences, Easy Eddie had the courage to make the right choice. In doing so, he left a powerful positive legacy that lived on in his son.

The life you live today affects the generations to come, even if you do not see it, and this is often the case when you coach others. A simple word of encouragement, a decision you make, or a stance you take can create a defining moment for someone you are coaching or someone who is simply observing you. Living a positive life and being a positive coach is the best way to leave a positive legacy.

> *If your actions create a legacy that inspires others to dream more, learn more, do more and become more, then you are an excellent leader.*
>
> **—DOLLY PARTON**
> Singer, Songwriter, Actress, Author, Producer, and Businesswoman

Inspiring winning results and relationships for your team is a leadership marathon that is won with daily sprints. If you maintain a positive coaching mindset and positive coaching habits daily, then victory is yours. You will predictably build a winning team and reap all the benefits it brings, personally and professionally. You have already taken the first step by reading this book. Now, take the next step and you're on your way!

ENDNOTES

INTRODUCTION. ELEVATE YOUR COACHING GAME

1. Kevin Cashman, "Leadership from the Inside Out: Eight Pathways to Mastery," Forbes.com, Oct. 8, 2017, https://www.forbes.com/sites/kevincashman/2017/10/08/leadership-from-the-inside-out-eight-pathways-to-mastery/#746cc11b549c

2. Norman Triplett, "The Dynamogenic Factors in Pacemaking and Competition," *The American Journal of Psychology* 9, no.4 (1898): 507–533, http://dx.doi.org/10.2307/1412188

PART I. POSITIVE COACHING MINDSET

1. Carol S. Dweck, *Mindset: The New Psychology of Success*, (New York: Ballantine Books, 2007).

2. Meghan Walsh, "Their Breakthrough Formula: Women CEOs," Korn Ferry Briefing Magazine, Feb. 2018, https://www.kornferry.com/institute/the-breakthrough-formula-women-ceos

3. P. Alex Linley, Linda Woolston, and Robert Biswas-Diener, "Strengths Coaching with Leaders," *International Coaching Psychology Review* 4(1) (2009): 37–48.

4. Barbara L. Fredrickson, Michael A. Cohn, Kimberly A. Coffey, Jolynn Pek, and Sandra M. Finkel, "Open Hearts Build Lives: Positive Emotions, Induced through Loving-Kindness Meditation, Build Consequential Personal Resources," *Journal of Personality and Social Psychology* 95(5) (2008): 1045–1062, http://dx.doi.org/10.1037/a0013262

CHAPTER 1. KNOW YOUR THOUGHTS

1. David Zes and Dana Landis, "A Better Return on Self-Awareness: Companies with Higher Rates of Return on Stock Also Have Employees with Few Personal Blind Spots," Proof Point, Korn/Ferry Institute, Aug. 2013.

CHAPTER 2. KNOW YOUR PURPOSE

1. Mac Anderson, and Lance Wubbels, *To a Child Love Is Spelled T-i-m-e: What a Child Really Needs from You* (Nashville, TN: FaithWords/Center Street, 2004).
2. Karen A. Jehn, and Priti Pradhan Shah, "Interpersonal Relationships and Task Performance: An Examination of Mediating Processes in Friendship and Acquaintance Groups," *Journal of Personality and Social Psychology* 72(4) (1997): 775–790.
3. Susan Ellingwood, "The Collective Advantage: Contrary to Popular Belief, Workplace Friendships Boost Profits," *GALLUP Business Journal* Online (Sept. 15, 2001), https://news.gallup.com/businessjournal/787/collective-advantage.aspx
4. Simone Schnall, Kent D. Harper, Jeanine K Stefanucci, and Dennis R. Proffitt, "Social Support and the Perception of Geographical Slant," *Journal of Experimental Social Psychology* 44 (2008): 1246–1255, Doi:10.1016/j.jesp.2008.04.011

CHAPTER 4. KNOW YOUR EMOTIONS

1. Andrea Ovans, "How Emotional Intelligence Became a Key Leadership Skill," *Harvard Business Review*, April 28, 2015, https://hbr.org/2015/04/how-emotional-intelligence-became-a-key-leadership-skill

2. Susan David, "You Can Write Your Way Out of an Emotional Funk. Here's How," *The Cut*, Sept. 6, 2016, https://www.thecut.com/2016/09/journaling-can-help -you-out-of-a-bad-mood.html

3. Sara D. Hodges, and Michael W. Myers in Roy F. Baumeister and Kathleen D. Vohs, eds. *Encyclopedia of Social Psychology*, (Thousand Oaks, CA: Sage Publications, 2007), http://dx.doi.org/10.4135/9781412956253.n179 http://pages.uoregon.edu/hodgeslab/files/Download /Hodges%20Myers_2007.pdf

4. Roman Krznaric, "5 Ways to be More Empathetic," Time.com, Nov. 6, 2014, http://time.com/3562863/ 5-ways-to-be-more-empathetic/

CHAPTER 5. POSITIVE COACHING HABIT #1:
EXPLAIN EXPECTATIONS TO GAIN ALIGNMENT

1. Peter Gollwitzer, "Goal Achievement: The Role of Intentions," *European Review of Social Psychology*, vol. 4 (Hoboken, NJ: John Wiley & Sons Ltd, 1993).

CHAPTER 6. POSITIVE COACHING HABIT #2:
ASK QUESTIONS TO IGNITE ENGAGEMENT

1. Andrew Levi, Chairman, Blue Calypso, personal interview, June 12, 2018.

2. Paul Spiegelman, former CEO of the Beryl Companies and Chief Culture Officer of Stericycle, personal interview, June 12, 2012.

CHAPTER 7. POSITIVE COACHING HABIT #3:
INVOLVE TEAM TO ENLIST OWNERSHIP

1. Bob Bunker, President and CEO of Lakeview Health, personal interview, Oct. 17, 2012.

2. Yasuda Yuzo, *40 Years, 20 Million Ideas: The Toyota Suggestion System* (New York: Productivity Press, 1990).

CHAPTER 8. POSITIVE COACHING HABIT #4:
MEASURE RESULTS TO BOOST ACCOUNTABILITY

1. John Walker, CFO of Vira Insight, personal interview, July 11, 2012.
2. Stephen Mansfield, CEO of Methodist Health System in Dallas, personal interview, May 8, 2018.
3. Sophie Curtis, "Spotify Deploys Salesforce Rypple for Social Enterprise," *Tech Advisor*, May 24, 2012, https;//www.techadvisor.co.uk/feature/small-business/spotify-deploys-salesforce-rypple-for-social-enterprise-3359744/?amp
4. Stephen R. Covey, *The 7 Habits of Highly Effective People*, (New York: Simon & Schuster, Sept. 1989).

CHAPTER 9. POSITIVE COACHING HABIT #5:
APPRECIATE PEOPLE TO DEEPEN COMMITMENT

1. Tom Rath and Donald O. Clifton, *How Full Is Your Bucket?* (New York: Gallup, 2004).
2. Ferdinand F. Fournies, *Why Employees Don't Do What They're Supposed to Do and What to Do About It* (New York: McGraw-Hill, 1999).
3. Daniel Jones, Chairman, President, and CEO of Encore Wire, personal interview, Jan. 27, 2017.

PART III. YOUR COACHING GAME PLAN

1. Harry McCracken, "Microsoft Rewrites the Code," *Fast Company*, Oct. 1, 2017, https://www.scribd.com/article/357616590/Microsoft-Rewrites-The-Code

REINFORCEMENT RESOURCES

Executive Coaching

The *Executive Navigation*^{SM} coaching process is results-focused and supported by field-tested tools to help you elevate your leadership. Clients measurably and significantly improve personal productivity and team performance.

Keynote Presentation

Invite the authors to present a high-energy, engaging look at how to coach for winning results and relationships by applying *The Power of Positive Coaching* concepts and tools.

High-Impact Workshop

Equip your organization's leaders with the tools to inspire winning results and relationships. Delivered by one of the authors or a certified facilitator, this high-impact, interactive workshop delivers actionable tools that participants can put to work right away.

Trainer's Kit

Train your leaders on *The Power of Positive Coaching*. This just-add-water training kit includes: detailed facilitator notes and engaging participant exercises, 70+ professionally designed slides that address key points from the book, 50+-page participant guide.

180-Degree Coaching Assessment

Elevate your coaching game! You and your team take this confidential, online assessment to provide you with a 180-degree view of your coaching effectiveness. Includes a detailed feedback report, reflection questions and a personal action plan.

Elevate Your Coaching Game at:
theLgroup.com
972-250-9989

For Free leadership tips and tools:
Text "leadership" to 444-999

INDEX

ABOUT THE AUTHORS

Lee J. Colan, PhD is a high-energy leadership advisor, engaging speaker, and popular author. He was nominated for the Thinkers50 Award for best management thinker globally. Lee has authored 15 popular leadership books, including two bestsellers that have been translated into 10 languages. His cut-through-the-clutter advice is anchored in his corporate leadership experience and robust consulting business.

Lee earned his doctorate in Industrial/Organizational Psychology from George Washington University, in Washington, DC, after graduating from Florida State University.

Julie Davis-Colan is an innovative business advisor and peak performance coach, with experience in sales and marketing to *Fortune 500* companies. Julie has coauthored six popular books. She has been coaching and encouraging positive behavior change for 30 years, with a focus on organizational health and peak performance. Additionally, Julie is a compelling speaker and engaging trainer. Her passion for leadership and life creates an infectious energy for audiences.

Julie earned her Master's degree in Preventive Medicine from The Ohio State University, College of Medicine, after graduating from Florida State University.

THE **L** GROUP
Leadership at every level.

 Consulting: Our top-notch consultants deliver cut-through-the-clutter insights that drive results for your team.

 Executive Coaching: Our advisors help executives boost team and personal performance.

 Speaking: Engage your team with passionate delivery and equip them with practical tools.

 Resources: Rapid-read books, multimedia training tools and leadership assessments.

 Training: Rely on our certified facilitators (English- or Spanish-speaking) or use our just-add-water training kits for internal delivery.

theLgroup.com   972.250.9989